Live-In Child Care

Live-In Child Care

THE COMPLETE GUIDE

BARBARA BINSWANGER
AND BETSY RYAN

A DOLPHIN BOOK
DOUBLEDAY & COMPANY, INC.
1986

Library of Congress Cataloging-in-Publication Data

Binswanger, Barbara.
  Live-in child care.

  "A Dolphin book."
  1. Child care services—United States. 2. Child
care workers—United States. 3. Child care services—
United States—Directories. I. Ryan, Elizabeth A.
(Elizabeth Anne), 1943–   . II. Title.
HQ778.7.U6B56 1986   362.7'12   86-13520
ISBN 0-385-23680-8
ISBN 0-385-23681-6 (pbk.)

Acknowledgments

It would be impossible to thank all the people who were so generous with their time, advice, and expertise but we would like to mention a few who were particularly helpful: Joy Shelton and Vicki Van Steenhouse of the American Council of Nanny Schools, Toni Porter of Child Care Inc., and Pat Ward of Catalyst. Our thanks, too, to Danielle Grado for her patient help in assembling the manuscript, to Paul Bresnick and Karen Suben, our editors at Doubleday, and finally to Jim Charlton for his editorial and moral support.

Contents

An overview of live-in and non-live-in child care options, including descriptions of professionally trained nannies, mother's helpers, summer helpers, au pairs, full-time baby-sitters, share care, family day providers, drop-in centers, baby-sitting co-ops, day care centers, corporate day care, postpartum care, and information and referral services.

Detailed checklists to help you evaluate your family's needs, including discussions of financial and logistical considerations, housekeeping requirements, emotional issues, and the specific needs of your child.

A closer look at the differences among American trained nannies, British trained nannies, "untrained" nannies or mother's helpers, and summer helpers.

How to locate and interview potential nannies and mother's helpers, including discussions of employment agencies, advertising, word of mouth, and interviewing in person and long-distance.

An explanation of U.S. immigration policies, hiring illegal foreign workers, "sponsoring" a worker, "green cards," hiring au pairs on tourist visas, getting au pairs into the United States, and two U.S. government sanctioned programs that allow you to hire au pairs legally.

How to prepare your home, yourself, and your family for your live-in helper's arrival, setting up "house rules," anticipating and defusing emotional issues such as jealousy or homesickness, and handling her departure.

How to negotiate and write a fair contract with your live-in helper, including discussions of salaries, overtime policies, vacations, holidays, the value of room and board, "paying off the books," child care tax credits, withholding taxes, Social Security and unemployment taxes, Workers' Compensation insurance, and medical and automobile insurance.

Listings of national information and referral services, corporate day care organizations, American nanny schools,

employment agencies, British nanny schools and placement agencies, U.S. Immigration and Labor Certification
offices, offices of the legal au pair programs, and addresses
of recommended newspapers for classified ads. Plus sample tax, immigration, and visa forms.

Introduction

Although there have always been women who have worked outside the home, the working mother used to be considered an anomaly, an odd exception to the rule of a two-parent family where the daddy went out to work and the mommy stayed home and took care of the children. Today's typical family looks different. Many families contain two adult wage earners, and the type of family that has grown the most quickly over the past twenty years is the one headed by the single parent. Statistics predict that by 1990 only one out of every four married women will be a full-time housewife.

Unfortunately, the options in child care for working—and nonworking—parents have not kept pace with the changing times. Most women we spoke with told us that finding good child care arrangements was one of the most difficult parts of becoming a new parent. And most agencies agreed that the demand for quality child care far outweighs the available supply.

Despite the overall shortage of services, however, there are a wide range of child care alternatives to choose from. This book, though, is focused on options in *live-in* child care, which more and more parents have come to see as one of the most convenient, efficient, and emotionally rewarding situations for themselves and their child(ren).

As you read on, you will learn about the advantages and disadvantages of each of the various live-in options available to American parents. You'll see how you can arrange the situation that suits you best; how to prepare your family and your household for a live-in worker; and how to sustain and develop a successful arrangement.

After seeing what's available, you may find that live-in child care is not after all the best option for your family. It's not for everybody. For the sake of comparison, we have discussed some out-of-home alternatives that will help you to make that decision.

But for those of you for whom live-in child care is right, this book will provide everything you need to know to design a satisfying and enriching arrangement.

It's important that you read the entire book. Every chapter has information that will be useful to you even at this early stage in your decision making, and some of that information may well change your thinking about the best live-in child care for you. It will certainly affect the way you handle the hiring and negotiating process and the way you prepare your household for your live-in helper's arrival.

Throughout this book you'll notice that we most often use the phrase "live-in helper"—rather than "nanny"—as the generic term. We've done this in order to differentiate between the professionally trained American and British nannies and other types of care givers, such as mother's helpers and au pairs. You should be aware, however, that many employment agencies use the term "nanny" to describe *any* live-in helper, even if she has no professional training. Most live-in helpers refer to themselves as nannies as well.

We also chose to use the personal pronoun "she" when referring to live-in helpers. There are some young men who choose this type of work (they're known as "mannies" in the trade), but the vast majority of live-in helpers are female. We spoke with some "mannies," and they and their families were quite pleased with their situation, but even in this age of softening sex stereotypes, most families still prefer to have a woman caring for their small children.

We interviewed a wide range of people while researching this book—parents, children, nannies, mother's helpers, "illegal" au pairs, attorneys, nanny school and employment agency directors, and countless government and industry officials. We hope that by giving you the best of their advice and experiences we can make the experience of live-in care a positive one for you and, most important, for your child.

Live-In Child Care

One

What's Available in Child Care?

In order to develop the child care arrangements that are right for your family, you first need to know what your options are. In this chapter you will find descriptions of most of the various types of live-in care. We also discuss the most widely available types of non-live-in care, so that you can compare the advantages and disadvantages of these with the live-in options, before deciding whether live-in child care is right for you. Even if you are already convinced that you want live-in care, do take the time to read through the other options. Being familiar with *all* the alternatives (and weighing their strengths and weaknesses) is the first step toward making a good decision.

LIVE-IN OPTIONS

Professionally Trained Nannies

When we hear the word "nanny," many of us may think of Mary Poppins, or of Juliet Mills's television "Nanny": a magical figure with a British accent and no-nonsense manner who charms the children into impeccable behavior while making no emotional demands on the household's adults.

In fact, today's nanny is more likely to be a young American woman between the ages of eighteen and twenty, trained in one of the more than two dozen nanny schools that have sprung up around the United States. British nannies still exist, of course, and can be hired by those U.S. families who prefer what is considered the more formal and less flexible behavior of the European nanny. Both types of nannies are trained child care professionals who have studied infant and child care, child development and psychology, nutrition, educational play, and child safety. Many have also studied family relations, which has equipped them with skills to help them to adapt to living in your home.

Nannies live in their employers' houses and usually work about a twelve-hour day. They are generally willing to prepare the children's meals, clean the children's rooms, and do the children's laundry. Some will also do additional housework, depending on the arrangements you make. Because of the great demand for nannies, they typically earn a starting salary of twelve to fifteen thousand dollars a year, plus room and board. "It's quite a lot of money, especially when you add in health insurance, Social Security, and all the other benefits," one mother told us. "But it's worth it when I think of the piece of mind I get from having another adult in my home to care for my child."

Some families, of course, can't afford to pay quite such a high price. And some don't want nannies for other reasons. "Frankly, the thought of a trained British nanny was a little intimidating to me," explained one mother. "I pictured her as someone who had already raised several children and had very firm ideas about the whole thing. I wanted to raise my child in my own way."

Many of the advantages and disadvantages of using professionally trained nannies are the same as those of using other kinds of live-in help. Parents reported both concerns over privacy and fears that their children might consider the nanny their "real mother." On the other hand, working mothers mentioned the enormous relief of having a child care arrangement that could accommodate changes in their work schedules, and the unexpected sickness of a child. "Our nanny is always there; I can always count on her," said one young mother we interviewed. "That means more than anything else to me."

Advantages

- Continual care provided by someone who is familiar to and with your child.
- Reliable care not affected by bad weather, traffic problems, or your child's sickness.
- Flexible care, can be accommodated to schedule changes.
- Care available during nonwork hours.
- Caretaker trained and educated.
- Caretaker especially selected to suit your children's needs.
- Caretaker who will help with some housework.

Disadvantages

- Expensive.
- Child-rearing approaches that may conflict with your own.
- Loss of privacy (true for any kind of live-in help).
- Emotional demands of another relationship (again, true for any kind of live-in help).

UNTRAINED NANNIES AND MOTHER'S HELPERS

A live-in child care worker may not be a trained professional like a nanny. She might be a woman who has raised a family of her own, or a college- or high-school-age girl who loves children, who is an experienced baby-sitter, or who has helped bring up younger brothers and sisters. Because these live-in workers are not trained, they generally receive lower salaries than nannies do. But they may be able to provide a similar kind of quality care for your child.

There are pros and cons to both older and younger women. An older woman, particularly one with lots of experience around children, can bring a maturity and stability to your home that a teenager is unlikely to match. On the other hand, like the professionally trained nanny, she may have firm child-rearing ideas which may or may not be compatible with your own. A younger woman offers energy, and perhaps more willingness to take direction from you. And you may find yourself more comfortable supervising her. You will have to consider the possible negative aspects of taking someone into your home who could turn out to be "another child" to you, particularly if this is her first time living away from home.

Another consideration with any live-in child care worker is the relative lack of supervision. "I decided to put Jamie in day care, where I knew other parents would be keeping an eye on what was going on," one mother told us. "Maybe I was too cautious, but I thought I'd worry too much about leaving him alone all day with one other person." This mother wasn't concerned so much with the safety of her child as about whether he was receiving the kind of educational play she wanted for him. Other mothers reported concerns about whether a live-in sitter would feel pressured to put her housework and cooking duties ahead of the needs of the child.

Finally, although these workers receive lower salaries, they also have a correspondingly higher turnover. Younger women in particular may view their work as temporary, a break before starting college or getting into the field they really want. As a result, a year is most often all that a young child care person will stay. Some parents expressed frustration that their households and their children's lives were disrupted periodically, as live-in workers left and new ones had to be found and broken in.

Advantages

- Caretaker with a flexible attitude toward child care, amenable to supervision (particularly if worker is young).
- Caretaker often more willing than a nanny to do light housework, thus freeing parents from these chores.
- Reliable care not affected by weather, traffic, or your child's sickness.
- Caretaker relatively less expensive than a nanny or other trained live-in worker.
- Care that can accommodate emergencies, available during nonwork hours.

Disadvantages

- Loss of privacy.
- Emotional demands (particularly if worker is young).

- Possible high turnover.
- Caretaker with no formal training may not offer educational stimulation like that which a trained nanny or professional day care center provides.
- Lack of home supervision.

SUMMER HELPERS

The summer helper is usually a young American woman of high school or college age. These girls take live-in child care jobs as an opportunity to see different parts of the country in a relatively cheap and protected way, or they may see these jobs as a chance to earn some money while still enjoying a "vacation" atmosphere. The tradition or network that has developed to place summer helpers makes this an attractive option for young girls—or occasionally boys—whose parents might be uneasy about other types of travel.

Ideas about what summer helpers are expected to do can be vague on both sides. "Our summer helper worked out well eventually," one parent told us. "But only after a couple of major blowups. She thought she was having a vacation that might include taking a couple of kids to the beach. We expected her to put in a regular day's work that fit our schedule. Finally we all had to sit down and talk it out." A young nanny, now happily placed with a family she enjoys, had the opposite experience as a high school summer helper. "I was ready to watch the kids, maybe help with the cooking, the dishes, even the laundry," she recalled. "But they really thought they'd hired a maid— and even a maid wouldn't have worked so hard! They actually had me helping them strip and refinish the floors in their new summer house." (See Chapter Six for suggestions on how both sides can make their expectations clear *before* anyone is hired!)

Advantages

- Very inexpensive live-in alternative.
- Caretaker usually agreeable and cooperative about doing things your way.
- Caretaker who might be an energetic companion for your child.
- Reliable care not affected by weather, traffic, or your child's sickness.
- Caretaker likely to do at least some housework, as negotiated.

Disadvantages

- Possible feeling that you've inherited another child.
- Situation limited to a few months.
- Caretaker's lack of formal training and/or education.
- Caretaker more interested in enjoying the vacation than in working.

Au Pairs

The idea of an au pair used to have the same fantasy quality as did that of the nanny. She was most often imagined as a sweet young woman who cooked three-star meals, kept the house in perfect order, and turned your children into bilingual paragons before she returned home to her country. But even more ordinary au pairs were becoming an extinct breed as immigration rules changed and U.S. work permits became harder to obtain. Recently, however, two programs were set up to legally bring in and place young British and English-speaking Europeans between the ages of eighteen and twenty-five with American host families for a twelve-month period. These women have secondary school diplomas or certificates, and some prior child care experience. Host families are responsible for various expenses, including tuition for some educational programs. (For more information on this, see Chapter Three.)

Other kinds of foreign-born help are available for live-in child care and light housework, but not always through strictly legal means. Women of various ages may seek American jobs in order to obtain visas or "green cards" that will enable them to continue working in the United States. These women will probably not have any formal training, and may not speak much English. However, they may be experienced and loving caretakers of children.

Advantages

- Perhaps the least expensive live-in alternative.
- Caretaker who is agreeable and cooperative about doing things your way.
- Caretaker who might be an energetic companion for your children.
- Reliable care not affected by weather, traffic, or your child's sickness.
- Caretaker likely to do at least some housework, as negotiated.
- Foreign culture and language exposure for your child and family.
- Flexible care, available during nonwork hours.

Disadvantages

- Possible legal problems with foreign-born students and other child care workers without green cards.
- Possible feeling that you've inherited another child.
- Strong likelihood of their homesickness, loneliness, difficulties in adjusting to new culture.
- Caretaker with lack of formal training, education.
- Loss of privacy for the family.
- Lack of home supervision.

BABY NURSES

One mother described a baby nurse as "the best alternative I can think of to a grandmother." In the absence of extended families new mothers often turn to the services of a baby nurse.

While these women are not usually registered nurses, they are trained in pediatrics and, in most cases, take care of all the needs of a newborn baby: bathing, dressing, cooking for, and feeding the child (the latter, of course, when a mother is not nursing). Since she is responsible for the total care of a new infant, a baby nurse is not expected to look after the needs of older siblings. She does, however, often take care of the new mother if time permits. Virginia Muhlberg, owner of the Finnish Employment Agency in New York, told us that the duties of the baby nurse can vary from household to household. "Some parents need or want someone whose sole job is taking care of the baby," she said, "while others want someone to look after the baby in addition to keeping house, which can include grocery shopping for the mother, cooking, and serving meals for the entire family."

As with most child care, mothers rely on word of mouth and recommendations of friends as much as on agencies to find a baby nurse. Ms. Muhlberg, whose agency does national placements, says that it's often difficult to find a baby nurse through an agency. "A lot of time we 'lose' our people," she told us, "because once we place them, they become part of a network and simply go from one assignment to another." Most mothers recommend neighborhood and community word of mouth as the best way to find a baby nurse. The most obvious source, of course, is tracking down recent new mothers for the names of baby nurses they had.

Mothers and placement agencies emphasized that it is

crucial to "reserve" a baby nurse well in advance of your delivery date. They suggest two or three months' notice as a minimum (one mother we spoke to was so concerned that she have a nurse for her first baby that she "reserved" one six months in advance).

A baby nurse expects to be hired for a minimum of one week and some stay with families for up to two months, but the average stay is around two or three weeks. They are paid anywhere from sixty to a hundred dollars a day, with the average salary falling somewhere around eighty dollars a day. Although a baby nurse lives in your house, she doesn't usually expect a separate bedroom, choosing instead to sleep in the same room as the baby. After all, she's being paid to respond to the 4 A.M. cries of the newborn—something you'll have ample opportunity to do after she leaves. (Postpartum care can offer some of the services of a baby nurse; see the listing under "Non-Live-In Options.")

Besides her salary, you're expected to pay for the baby nurse's transportation to and from your house on her day off (which is normally one of every seven days she spends with you). An additional expense is the agency fee which is usually 18 percent of one month's salary or 10 percent of the salary if she stays less than a month.

While a baby nurse can be a comforting and reassuring presence to a new mother, some parents are intimidated by the wealth of experience and knowledge that the nurse brings to her job. One mother told us about someone she hired who insisted on being referred to as a "baby technician," and although she was competent, her presence was very grating. This was in direct contrast to the loving, gentle woman whom the mother had found for her first baby, someone, she said, "I wanted to keep around for the rest of my life."

Advantages

- Continual care for newborn.
- Specially trained caretaker to give support where necessary.
- New mother enabled to recuperate and regain strength.
- Family stress lessened by extra help.

Disadvantages

- Expensive.
- Loss of privacy (true for any live-in help).
- Infant care approach may differ from your own.
- Feelings of intimidation on part of the new mother (especially new first-time mothers).

NON-LIVE-IN OPTIONS

BABY-SITTERS

Of course, the time-honored means of child care is simply to hire someone to come to your house to take care of your child for a specified number of hours. (Or, in some cases, to take your child to that person's house for hourly child care.) Working parents need sitters on whom they can rely for a specified number of hours per week, over a reasonably lengthy period of time. If you choose this method of child care, it's a good idea to have as many backup systems as you can manage. Sitters might get sick, run into emergencies of their own, or face weather/transportation problems in getting to your house (or you to theirs); "what to do when the sitter can't come" was a frequent theme we heard in many of our conversations with working mothers. Also, sitters' lives can change; unlike, for example, a day care center, which is probably not going to go out of business, sitters frequently decide that they are unable or unwilling to continue taking care of your child. If you've got a friend, neighbor, drop-in center, or other arrangement lined up for that frequent gap between sitters, you'll be in much better shape.

Many families we spoke with had exceptionally good luck finding warm, dedicated sitters who developed close and lasting relationships with the children for whom they cared. You will need to see that a daily sitter, who is alone with your child all day, gets the same kind of supervision from you as would a live-in sitter, but if you take the same kinds of precautions with supervision and references, you can establish a good situation for you and your child.

Most people we spoke with found their sitters by word of mouth, which also helped build trust into the relationship from the beginning. Some families advertised for a sitter in local or community papers, or had responded to an ad in a paper or on a community bulletin board. Everyone agreed that good sitters are hard to find and often hard to keep, but that if successful, the search was well worth the trouble.

Advantages

- Child care in your child's own home, or in another home environment.
- Continuity of care with a single care giver.
- Sitters sometimes flexible about coming early or staying late.
- Far less expensive than live-in help, generally less expensive than day care.
- More parental control over their child-rearing philosophy than is the case with a day care center.

Disadvantages

- Possibility of sitters getting sick, facing an emergency, or being unable to reach your house.

- Possibility of sitters being late in arriving.
- Turnover rate often very high.
- Depending on the salary offered, possibility of a less well-educated person taking care of your child.
- Lack of supervision.

SHARE CARE

An increasingly popular form of day care, "share care," is an arrangement where parents pool their resources to hire a qualified child care worker. If two to four families share the cost, they can afford to pay a more reasonable salary than any one family could afford to pay alone. The children can be cared for in the home of the child care worker, or they can rotate among the families' homes, which allows them to remain in a home environment, rather than in the schoollike atmosphere of a regular day care center.

One working mother told us that her share care arrangement proved to be a real godsend. "I wouldn't have felt right about paying someone $2.00 to $3.00 an hour to watch my child," she explained, "and we just couldn't afford to pay any more. With the other two families, we each put in $2.50 per hour and our sitter got $7.50 an hour for watching three children. She was happy and we were happy."

If you are considering share care arrangements, remember that they can be a lot of work. Any time one family changes its schedule or decides to find another day care service, the other families involved have to readjust, possibly covering increased costs for a period of time. Of course, there is rarely a shortage of families seeking child care, but taking the time to reestablish the share care relationship can be frustrating. "When one of our families dropped out, I was in a real bind," admitted the working mother we just quoted. "I think I spent four solid hours on the phone that night, and I was frantic. Luckily we found someone else within a week because I don't know how we could have kept on paying the increased rate."

Advantages

• Particularly suitable arrangement for infants and for other children who require a home environment.
• Relatively inexpensive.
• Arrangement that provides some flexibility.

Disadvantages

• Difficulty in finding the right group of parents.
• Arrangement provides no one to do housework.
• Turnover in both the families and child care workers possibly a problem.

FAMILY DAY CARE PROVIDERS

These are women—not necessarily mothers—who are trained in child care by a family day care network in your county. They take care of children in their own homes and are provided with toys, a children's library, and equipment by the network. The women are certified and licensed by the state. Although there is no national family day care network to guarantee the standards of care, the women do meet the minimum standards of their local communities. The training requirement varies in each community.

Family Day Care was started more than twenty years ago and is today the most common out-of-the-home care in the country. As the cost for infant and toddler care increases, this type of care is becoming even more popular, since most day care centers don't accept children below the age of two or three.

Parents usually leave their children in a family day care home from 8 A.M. to 6 P.M., for a fee of approximately forty-five dollars for a five-day week. Some of these homes are available for extended hours or days; for example, stewardesses in Atlanta working three-day shifts can arrange to have their babies cared for over that time. Most family day care centers care for five to ten children at a time.

To find a family day care provider near you, look in your local telephone directory under Child Care Coordinating Council. You might find the listing in either the white or the yellow pages, under either the council's name or the listings for your county. If you can't find a listing in your local directory, one of the Information and Referral Services in the Appendix may be able to help you. The council matches you with a provider convenient to your neighborhood or place of work, but it will be up to you to see if this is an appropriate arrangement for your child.

Advantages

- Very reasonable price.
- Child care worker who is trained.
- Home environment for your child, plus equipment and library that are unusual in most homes.
- Flexibility of extended hours in some cases.
- Some supervision.

Disadvantages

- Varying degrees of supervision and standards of care.
- Extra time added to your daily commute to drop off and pick up your child.
- Possibility of less stimulation and variation than at a day care center, because each home has only a single provider.
- Lack of any advantages of live-in help regarding housework.

Drop-In Home Centers

A drop-in home center is usually run by a woman with a lot of experience in caring for children, or with one or two small children of her own. More flexible than a day care center, the drop-in home center allows parents to bring children in for care at any time during daytime hours, charging parents for only the time the children are actually there. Some parents use drop-in centers as a backup to fill in the gaps between regular arrangements, in cases of schedule changes, or on days when the regular child care worker is sick. Other parents rely regularly on this arrangement.

Many parents told us that the drop-in centers had saved their lives more than once in an emergency, but that they would not care to use them on a regular basis. Some were concerned that their children might not receive enough individual attention because of the number of other children. Others wanted their children to have more consistent educational activities, such as those provided by trained child care workers or at day care centers.

Advantages

- Flexible arrangement requiring no ongoing commitment of money or time.
- Care for infants or children too young to be left in a regular day care center.
- Children allowed to socialize with other children while remaining in a home environment.
- Cost usually fairly low, because more than one family is served.
- Caretakers with experience with many children, they may be mothers themselves.

Disadvantages

- Possible lack of ongoing individual attention to or edu
cational play with your child.
- Less supervision than in-home care, with less formal
training than day care centers.

BABY-SITTING CO-OPS

If you are a parent with a flexible schedule and know
other parents whose time is flexible too, you may want to
organize a baby-sitting co-op. This kind of arrangement is
especially popular with parents who work part-time, at
irregularly scheduled jobs, or who go to school. A number
of parents, for example, four or five to begin with, agree to
pool their time and child care energies. When a sitter is
needed, a parent telephones the "co-op secretary," a ro-
tating position taken by each parent for a month at a time.
The secretary then calls around among the other parents
to find someone willing to take the first parent's children
for the specified time. The secretary keeps track of how
much time each parent "owes" the co-op, so that everyone ends up contributing the same amount of baby-sitting
time over the life of the co-op.

This kind of arrangement is clearly not feasible for
someone who requires nine-to-five coverage every week.
But parents we spoke with reported that it works extremely well for those with limited out-of-home commitments. "I had a standing request for Tuesday and Thursday afternoons, when my classes met," one mother
explained, "and then I'd use the co-op every other weekend or so, just to have some time to myself. The rest of the
time I was with my own children anyway, so it was usually
no more trouble to watch one or two more. In fact, sometimes it's easier to take someone else's children—then
yours have someone to play with."

A baby-sitting co-op requires an initial investment of organizational work, plus the additional task of being co-op secretary every few months. Parents must meet at least occasionally to set ground rules for their organization, deciding such questions as whether sitters can shop or run errands with the children, or how many hours a parent is allowed to "owe" at one time. However, you have the reassurance of knowing that your children are being cared for by other parents whom you know, and the freedom of flexible child care.

Advantages

- No cost.
- Parents likely to feel comfortable with the person caring for their child.
- Child provided with a chance to be with other adults and other children.
- Flexible arrangement.

Disadvantages

- Organizational work required to keep co-op going.
- Limited number of hours of use.
- Disagreements with other parents about child-rearing philosophies often harder to settle than those with hired child care workers.

DAY CARE CENTERS

The number of day care centers is growing, but they still offer vastly fewer places than will accommodate the number of parents who want them. There is currently room for about 1.2 million children in day care centers—about 12 percent of the children who need day care. One mother from the Boston area told us about a highly desirable Cambridge day care center that she claims is harder to get into than Harvard! Not all day care centers carry such prestige, but the better ones often have long waiting lists.

Most day care centers will not accept children under the age of two, although an increasing number of nurseries are becoming available to serve working parents of very young children. Day care centers usually require ongoing financial commitments from parents, generally by the month or semester, so that you pay for a certain number of scheduled hours whether or not your child actually attends the center for all of those hours. Day care centers are generally not flexible about time, requiring that children be picked up at the close of the day, regardless of a parent's sudden work emergency. Some day care centers have vacations—usually timed to coincide with school vacations—during which you must make other arrangements for your child. Most day care centers won't accept children when they are sick.

Those disadvantages of day care centers are well known. On the other hand, parents with children in day care centers have told us that the experience is quite positive for their children, offering a combination of educational play and opportunities for socializing that the children could find nowhere else. "Lissa has always been a happy, outgoing child," one mother told us. "But I've noticed that since she started going to the day care center, she's much calmer as well. It's as though all that activity and all those other kids give her an outlet for her energy."

Advantages

- Supervised, educational care.
- Equipment, supplies, and facilities offered not available in home care.
- A help for a child to get used to a schoollike environment.
- For the agreed-upon hours, extremely reliable arrangement.

- Contact provided for the child with a wide variety of children.

Disadvantages

- Although less costly than live-in help, still fairly expensive.
- Caretaking available only during certain hours, inflexible.
- Prior financial commitment required, regardless of the number of hours a child actually attends.
- Usually not available for children under the age of two.
- Centers sometimes hard to find, long waiting lists.
- Widely varying quality from center to center.
- Possible time-consuming commute to center.
- Usually not available to sick children.

CORPORATE DAY CARE

As more parents continue to work, companies are beginning to realize that day care can be an attractive benefit that increases productivity and boosts employee morale as well. Currently some twenty-five hundred U.S. companies provide on-site day care, so that employed parents have only a single commute and can often visit their children during the day. Other companies provide such child care benefits as reduced rates in local centers or baby-sitting referral services. Flextime, job-sharing, and part-time work with no loss of benefits are other corporate accommodations to parents who work.

Parents who use corporate day care are quite enthusiastic. It is often subsidized by the company, costing far less than other centers would charge. Some corporate sites also offer infant care to encourage employees to return to work sooner than two years after the birth. As you might expect, corporate day care centers have long waiting lists too, sometimes even longer than those of regular centers.

"I heard about one woman's pregnancy before her husband did," said one corporate day care center director. "She wanted to be *sure* to save a place for her child!"

Since a growing number of businesses are setting up corporate day care sites, any interested corporation can contract an experienced company, delegating the problem of starting the center to them. Many schools, universities, and hospitals have developed their own centers, drawing on existing resources to serve a largely female work force. Union contracts are increasingly demanding corporate contributions to day care, whether in the form of actual on-site centers, vouchers, or credits. If you are lucky enough to work for a company offering a day care plan, you've probably gone a long way toward solving your child care problems.

Advantages

- Convenient; child goes to day care where parent works.
- Relatively inexpensive, as low as fifteen dollars per week in some companies.
- Children available for the parents during the day.
- Frequent acceptance of infants and very young children.
- All the other advantages of regular day care provided.

Disadvantages

- Possible long waiting lists.
- Center hours not coinciding with your own. (They're often not open after 5 P.M. which could conflict with your work schedule—or unexpected work problems.)
- Parental preference for a home environment or more individualized care for the child.

Postpartum Care

For many new parents, the difficulties of finding day care are nothing compared to the stress of those first few days of taking care of a new baby. The first weeks of parenthood can be a joyful and affectionate time, as mother, father, and child develop new bonds. But as the new parents awaken for the fourth or fifth time at night to feed or comfort their baby, they may wish for some extra moral and physical support! Traditionally, relatives or friends came to help out for those first few weeks, doing the cooking or the housework, or sharing some of the late-night care, so that the mother and father would have more energy for caring for themselves, each other, and the baby.

Now there are professional services to provide postpartum care as well. Combining the skills of infant care, counseling, housekeeping, and just being a friend, the home care worker acts as a surrogate family member to help parents adjust to being home with their newborn.

"Postpartum care gave my husband and me a chance to spend more time with our other two children," one mother of three explained to us. "We had time to bond with the new one, but the extra help gave us the margin we needed to pay special attention to our first two as well." Postpartum services may be run by nurses, mid-wives, or lay specialists, offering a variety of services from routine checkups to full-time care. Most workers charge between ten and fifteen dollars per hour for preparing meals, doing light housekeeping and laundry, caring for older children, running errands, and generally being available to the family. Families use the service for three or four hours per day, up to about ten days after bringing the baby home.

Advantages

- Experienced child care worker available to offer advice and answer questions about infant care and postpartum feelings.
- Time made available for recovery, and for family.
- Some "mothering" provided to the mother which can help stave off postpartum depression.

Disadvantages

- Difficulty in adapting to another adult's presence at this emotional time.
- Cost possibly too expensive for some families already facing large obstetrics bills.

INFORMATION AND REFERRALS

Most parents told us that their greatest concern over child care was how they could know whether to trust the child care worker they selected. And, they reported, their greatest anxiety was the fear that they were missing sufficient information and passing up the child care option that was perfect for them simply because they had not happened to find out about it.

To alleviate these fears, profit and nonprofit information and referral services are springing up across the country. Also known as "R & R's"—for "Resource and Referrals"—Information and Referrals (I & R's) give out information about existing child care in a community, as well as help to develop new facilities. If you are searching for information about child care options in your area, you might consider writing or phoning an I & R for help. (For specific listings, see the Appendix.)

As you go on to read about the details of finding and living with live-in help, keep in mind all of the various live-in options—as well as the alternative kinds of care. You may find that an option you had never considered before will be better for you than the one you initially had in mind. In any case, now that you know what's available you're in a much better position to make a decision. The next step is to decide what you, your family, and your child *need*.

Two

Is Live-In Child Care Right for You?

For many families, a full-time live-in nanny, au pair, or mother's helper is the perfect answer to their child care needs, a solution that is rewarding to the parents, the helper, and the children. But because live-in care will bring more changes into your day-to-day life than will out-of-the-home care or daily sitters, you need to give some serious thought to whether it is the right choice for your family.

A live-in helper will certainly allow you more flexibility and spontaneity in your life, but the reverse side of this is the inevitable intrusion on your privacy. Will the benefits of live-in help be worth the emotional demands of another household resident? Do the details of working out a business relationship with a single caretaker seem preferable to the ongoing monitoring of out-of-the-home care?

Working out any successful arrangement means considering the different relationships that each child care option implies: with another person living in your house; with a person who comes and goes in your house; with another mother caring for your children in her home; or with a paid, professional day care staff. Obviously, a relationship with a live-in helper will be the most intimate and involved of these. Carefully weighing the advantages and disadvantages of each of the options will make you more comfortable with whatever decision you ultimately make.

The first step is to identify and evaluate your needs. As you think about your child care requirements, it's useful to break down your priorities into five areas: financial, logistical, and emotional needs, the needs of your child, and the housekeeping requirements. Once you've determined what's most important, you will be able to decide whether live-in help is right for you and your family.

FINANCIAL CONSIDERATIONS

How do money and the family budget affect your child care decisions? Decide how much you can afford to spend on child care before you have to start cutting back in other areas. How do child care expenses affect the other ways you will want to spend money on your child, such as outings, music lessons, and other "extras"? What can you realistically afford to spend on child care. Would you consider cutting back on other items that mean a lot to your family, such as vacations, eating out, or other family activities? You may want to come up with a minimum and maximum figure for your child care budget to give you some idea of the financial trade-offs when you're looking at various types of child care.

As you compare the expense of live-in help to other types of child care, make sure you take all the various costs into account. If you pay any sitter more than fifty dollars over three months, you are required to file to pay Social Security. Some child care expenses can be offset by the Child Care Credit on your federal income taxes, but in order to claim the credit you have to have a record of paying for the care. Paying someone "off the books," whether it be a live-in nanny, daily sitter, or someone who takes children into her home, will not give you the documentation you need to claim the tax credit. (See Chapter Seven for more details.)

The salaries for live-in help run from seventy-five dollars per week for a young au pair or mother's helper to three hundred or more per week for a professionally trained or highly experienced nanny. This is, of course, in addition to room and board, an expense that you should not take lightly. Will you have to spend money fixing up your live-in sitter's accommodations? Make sure you calculate the cost of another adult using the telephone, the electricity, the hot water, and so forth. Some parents were surprised to find that their telephone bill rose by 20 percent after their helper's arrival.

You will have to make some accommodation in your food budget for another person's tastes or habits. If your family belongs to clubs where you frequently take the children, you may have to pay for an additional membership. You should think about how you will handle family excursions to movies or the zoo, and how you plan to handle the sitter's expenses for such trips. If you need a sitter to accompany you and the children on out-of-town travel, you will have to pay further transportation and lodging expenses. It is not just her salary you have to consider, but a number of less apparent expenses as well. Think through all the different situations in which you imagine using a live-in sitter, and try to come up with a realistic budget for expenses beyond salary, room, and board. (See Chapter Seven for further guidelines and information.)

Finally, don't forget the costs of finding child care help. If you advertise in a newspaper, or register with an agency, there will be bills to pay. Most agencies charge somewhere between two weeks of a nanny's or mother's helper's salary and 10 percent of her annual pay. If you are "importing" your nanny or au pair you will most likely be expected to cover her transportation expenses as well. And if your nanny or sitter gets sick, doesn't work out, or suddenly takes another job, you'll have to figure in the costs of paying for child care elsewhere while you look for a replacement.

Following is a short checklist of points for you to consider if finances are a prime consideration:

FINANCIAL NEEDS CHECKLIST

- What is the most I can afford to pay for child care without cutting back on other activities?
- What is the most I can afford to pay for child care if I *do* cut back on other activities? Where will these cuts come from? (You may want to make a list of several different options against which you can compare your later research on child care costs.)
- Is my family income irregular in any way, due to freelance work, overtime, or business factors? How will this affect my ability to pay for child care on a daily, weekly, monthly, or quarterly basis?
- Do I have the kind of job where I lose money if I stay home with my sick child? What are the financial costs of

staying home versus those of paying for child care arrangements that will work with a sick child?

• Do I have access to other affordable backup help to "fill in the gaps" in my arrangements—a neighbor, friend, or relative available on short notice and low cost? Or must I budget more for more flexible and extensive arrangements?

LOGISTICAL CONSIDERATIONS

For a number of families, the financial aspects of child care are not the key consideration; for them it is more a matter of logistics. With some family schedules, live-in care is the only option that makes good sense. Run through your choices once again to see if they can accommodate your schedule. Even if other options are a possibility, you may still feel that you prefer the flexibility of live-in help.

Start by picturing your workday and the demands it makes on your time. Do you need to have *absolutely reliable* help from nine to five because you can't afford to be even five minutes late to work? Are you interested in a child care arrangement that will allow you to work unexpected overtime, or to take a spontaneous evening out? Will your schedule accommodate the daily commute to and from a day care center or drop-off sitter? Is there a day care center or sitter that is reasonably convenient? Is it important to have child care combined with housework arrangements, to free you from a few of your household chores? Do you have the option of staying home with a sick child? What if your daily sitter couldn't work because of an emergency or illness?

Good backup possibilities to day care or sitters may make them palatable, no matter how tight your schedule. If you've got a relative who's happy to take your child on short notice, or if there is a drop-in home in your neighborhood that will do in a pinch, you might not mind some uncertainty in your arrangements. If, on the other hand, you're a single parent with an erratic schedule, you may prize flexibility in child care above all else.

Obviously a live-in helper can provide the most flexible and reliable arrangement. But before you hire one, you still must consider your household logistics. Can you provide a live-in helper with her own room? The rare helper who is willing to share quarters with a child will do so only while the child is an infant.

Think about your household routine. Must your live-in helper be able to drive? Could you provide her with a car or would she have to supply her own? Even if you don't need a driver, she will still need access to some kind of transportation for socializing. Do you have pets? You'll require a helper who doesn't mind or likes animals. If you have a backyard pool, you'll want someone who is a good swimmer. Asking yourself questions like these will help you to better define the qualities you'll need in a live-in helper.

We've covered some of the points you should consider when weighing the options of in-the-home versus out-of-the-home child care. Here is a checklist of questions:

Logistical Needs Checklist

- What is the physical space like in your household? Will it comfortably accommodate a live-in helper? Will it allow her—and the rest of you—sufficient privacy? Can you offer a live-in helper a separate entrance or sitting room, her own refrigerator or kitchenette? Can you at least offer her the basic minimum of a comfortable bedroom and bath?
- Do you have requirements for age, experience, or prior training?
- Do you prefer a nonsmoker?

- Should she have a driver's license?
- Should your helper be able to swim or be trained in water safety?
- What is your family routine like? Would having live-in help affect your entertaining?
- Would live-in help affect your travel or vacation routines?
- Do you and your partner have similar schedules (that is, you both are gone from nine to five), or overlapping ones (one of you works weekends, nights, or travels for work irregularly)? How does this affect your child care needs? Do you need child care so that you and your husband can spend time together?
- What are your needs for "recreational" as opposed to "work-related" child care? Do you need the same child care arrangements to meet both needs?
- How flexible is your work schedule? Do you have expected or unexpected schedule changes such as overtime or late work?
- Do you or your partner work a shift that precludes certain kinds of day care?
- How do you and your partner get to work each day? Will your schedules accommodate a trip to the day care center or drop-off sitter?
- How would a daily sitter get to your house? Are you accessible by public transportation? Would the weather in your area make a sitter's travel to your house unpredictable? Can your schedules accommodate that?
- Is help with the housework an important requirement to you?
- What are the language requirements for a sitter? From a logistical point of view, do you require someone in your house to take phone messages, deal with deliveries, or do other work that a non-English speaker might find difficult? (Of course, you will also be taking your child's needs into account in this regard.)

- What kind of backup do you have—neighbors, friends, relatives, local teenagers? How do these affect your child care requirements?
- Do you have pets that need daily attention? Might your live-in helper be put off by fear, allergies, or responsibilities involving the pet?

HOUSEWORK REQUIREMENTS

If you are hiring someone to do housework as well as child care, you face another whole set of issues. How will you feel about her doing things differently from "your way"? This might not be a problem at all. As one single father told us, "Since housework was not my strong suit, *any* help I got was wonderful."

It will be important, however, for you to have a realistic idea of how much you can expect from your live-in helper and to decide what your priorities are. A spotless house? Do you care if the house is a mess if it meant that your child had a wonderful afternoon making a tent in the living room? You probably won't find someone who can keep your house in perfect order *and* give lots of quality time to your child, so you need to think about which is really important to you. Some women have fantasies about a live-in helper who will do everything that they themselves could never quite manage; they want to hire an idealized form of themselves. Other women want their housekeepers to be as committed to the household as they are themselves, forgetting that both housework and child care are difficult enough when it's your own house and your own child. Several employment agency directors told us that the most difficult parents to please were single mothers. Because they had such high expectations for themselves they were rarely satisfied with household work done by the live-in helper.

Try to be realistic. How much housework can you accomplish with a two-year-old underfoot all day? You *do* have the right to expect your child care worker to give her full attention to your child while she is working for you; and to expect a housekeeper to complete certain agreed-upon chores. Just be sure that both of you understand and agree ahead of time on what you expect. A number of child care agencies suggest—and even provide —a detailed written contract that spells out the housekeeping duties.

If you decide on live-in help, you will have to be clear about what you expect. It's all too easy, once someone is living in your home, to assume that she is "on call" twenty-four hours a day. You need to agree in advance on the specific hours of work, and on what constitutes "reasonable" flexibility—one late night a week? two? five? Late meaning seven o'clock? Ten o'clock? Midnight? A number of mothers feel that more than two late nights (usually after nine or nine-thirty) a week is too much to ask. Likewise, you need to determine how much housework you expect to be done. Most nannies and mother's helpers will prepare meals for the kids, keep the children's rooms neat, and do the children's laundry. Beyond that, you should be prepared to specify what you expect. It's not a good idea to cover everything with the phrase "light housework," which might mean anything from picking up the living room to dusting and vacuuming every room in a three-story house!

Here is a checklist of typical household tasks. All of these won't be important, nor will all of them get done unless you are hiring a full staff of servants. But consider each.

HOUSEWORK REQUIREMENTS CHECKLIST

How important is it to you that your child care helper do the following? How often?

- LAUNDRY
  ——Family and children's
  ——Children's only
- IRONING
  ——Family and children's
  ——Children's only
- GENERAL CLEANING
  ——Windows
  ——Floors (mopping and/or waxing)
  ——Dusting
  ——Bathrooms
  ——Vacuuming
- KITCHEN CLEANING
  ——Dishes
  ——Silver
  ——Taking out garbage
- COOKING
  ——Breakfast: Family and children's? Children's only?
  ——Lunch
  ——Dinner
- MAKING BEDS
  ——Children's only
  ——Family and children's
- MOWING THE LAWN/CLIPPING SHRUBBERY/WEEDING
- SHOPPING, RUNNING ERRANDS, DRIVING TO ACTIVITIES AND APPOINTMENTS

EMOTIONAL CONCERNS

All mothers agree that any child care arrangement makes emotional demands; after all, someone else will be taking care of your child for a good part of the day. You'll want a close, ongoing relationship with that person or those people, whether the care takes place in your home or outside of it.

Anyone you hire is going to have to be allowed a certain amount of freedom to do things her way. If the care takes place in your own home, you will, of course, have more control and be able to set the basic limits and the ground rules. You will have tried to find someone who's in basic agreement with your own philosophy of child raising, but for many hours each day that person will be on her own. She will need your trust and support to be able to take care of your child the way you would if you were home.

Whom will you be the most comfortable giving this independence to? Another resident of your household? A paid, professional day care worker outside your home? Another mother of small children, caring for your child along with her own? A daily sitter hired to work in your house? How will you feel if you have to disagree with the caretaker? Will you be more intimidated by a professional day care teacher than by a live-in helper? Are you confident in your ability to "check up" on a daily sitter working alone in your home with no supervision? Whatever kind of care you select, but especially with a live-in helper, it's important that you feel comfortable enough with the caretaker so that you can trust her and express your concerns. The two of you should have a comfortable give-and-take relationship, not always an easy plateau to reach.

The kind of relationship you have with your live-in helper will depend not only on her temperament, and yours, but on her age as well. An older helper could be comforting, intimidating, or maddeningly rigid, depending upon your own frame of mind. Age also determines to a large degree how close your personal relationship with the caretaker will be. The older she is, the less need she will probably have to be treated like "part of the family."

If the person you hire is quite young, you may find yourself with another "child" to care for, particularly if she's a foreigner who is lonely, homesick, or having trouble with the language. One Norwegian girl assured her employers that she was the independent type. Even her parents confirmed this to the family. But four weeks after her arrival, the girl flew home because she was homesick. Some mothers also worry that with young helpers they will have to contend with suitors, romances, and young men under foot, or that the young helper might prove attractive to their husbands. One suburban mother was stunned when her forty-two-year-old husband eloped with the nineteen-year-old au pair. While this is a rare occurrence, we did hear of a number of instances of young men coming to call on the young helpers.

Some mothers struggle with feelings of jealousy when the child runs to the live-in helper—instead of them—for comfort. A few live-in helpers reported working for mothers who had a hard time turning the homemaking, child-rearing role over to someone else and felt tempted to prove that no one could do their jobs as well as they could.

Obviously any of these feelings can complicate a live-in relationship. Will they pose problems for you and, if so, how you might deal with them? Again, being clear about your expectations ahead of time will go a long way toward preventing problems later on.

Here are some of the emotional issues you should ponder.

EMOTIONAL CONCERNS CHECKLIST

- What kind of relationship do you want with a live-in nanny or mother's helper? A "one of the family" type or a more businesslike arrangement?
- If your prospective mother's helper is quite young, will you be able to deal with the possibility of "another child" in the family?
- Will you find it difficult seeing your child develop a close relationship with another caretaker?

- How will you feel about another woman in your home doing work that you used to do?
- Will you be comfortable supervising an employee? Will you be able to drop in on her unexpectedly, or to find some other way of assuring yourself that she's providing your child with good care?
- When considering a live-in helper, how do you rate your desires for family privacy against the flexibility a live-in might provide?
- Is the helper's religion a consideration for you, since she'll be spending a significant amount of time with your child?

YOUR CHILD'S NEEDS

Most children are resilient creatures, able to adapt to a wide variety of situations as long as they know that their primary caretaker—you, and perhaps your partner— loves them and is there for them. It's very likely that your child *could* do well in any of a number of different child care situations. It's also true that you don't want just an *acceptable* arrangement. You want the *best possible* arrangement.

Think about your expectations for your child's care. Of course, you want a warm, loving atmosphere that will provide reasonable discipline and lots of interesting, stimulating new experiences. But beyond that, what do you want for your child? Do you value educational instruction? If so, will live-in help meet your needs, or is a day care center more likely to provide "classroom" activities? Is it most important to you that your child get lots of individual attention? Do you prefer that your child have close relationships with only a few primary caretakers? Or perhaps you're more concerned that he or she learns to socialize with other children? Do you want your child to be able to invite friends to your house? Are you interested in giving your child exposure to a wide range of children from different backgrounds? Each of these considerations will help you decide whether a day care center, a drop-in center, a daily sitter, or live-in help is most appropriate for you.

What is your own philosophy of child raising? You might not have thought it through, but you undoubtedly have one. How strong are your feelings about areas of child care such as play activities, food, television, safety, punishment, and respect. Do you generally feel comfortable with your child facing sets of habits and rules different from yours, or are you firmly rooted in your own particular way of doing things? Are there any aspects of child rearing where you have markedly different ideas than do many other people? If you have very specific ideas about how children should be disciplined or what type of play is appropriate, you may prefer a live-in helper whom you can supervise to a day care center with its own way of doing things.

Whatever your reasons for hiring live-in help, you should consider the type of person who would be best for your child. A young woman who can toss a baseball may be a better choice for an energetic three-year-old than an older woman with grown children.

But remember that your child's most basic need is the most important consideration of all. In the final analysis, you'll want to remember what most mothers told us: "I just want to find someone who will love my child." Love and affection toward the child is the prime requisite when evaluating any kind of child care.

Here is a checklist of points concerning your child's needs. Of all the checklists, this is the most important.

Your Child's Needs Checklist

- Do you have a particular method of discipline that's best for your child? What degree of discipline would you be comfortable in handing over to your child's care-taker?
- Is it important for your child to meet children from a variety of backgrounds?
- How important is it for your child to socialize in groups? (This is an especially important consideration for children who tend to be shy.)
- Does your child need a lot of individual attention?
- Would your child be uncomfortable in the unfamiliarity of another home, or adapt to a home setting not necessarily his or her own?
- Would your child benefit most from an institutional program that includes development of intellectual and language skills?
- How important is it to you for your child to have access to classroom materials?
- Do you want your child to have access to playground equipment? How often?
- How important is it for your child to develop self-help skills and independence?
- Do you have strong feelings about types of food?
- Is your child on a special diet, such as a vegetarian one?
- Do you have any rules about the amount or kind of television your child may watch?
- Should your child be able to invite friends home?
- Is it all right for your child to have play dates at other friends' houses?
- Does your child have any special health considerations such as diabetes, hemophilia, hyperactivity, or a disability of any kind?

- Should special care be given to educational needs, such as learning or developmental disabilities?
- Does your child have any special emotional needs or behavior problems?
- Does your child need to be driven to activities or appointments?

While leaving your child with another person is always an emotional experience, now that you have a clearer idea of what you need, what's available, and what you can afford, you should be able to make a decision that will satisfy your entire family.

If you now feel sure that live-in child care is for you, remember that finding the *right* live-in helper requires an investment of time and energy. In the chapters that follow, you'll learn how to find, hire, and live with each of the various kinds of live-in helpers. If you follow the advice in these chapters, you will be a long way ahead in your search.

Three

Nannies and Mother's Helpers

Baron von Trapp's children in *The Sound of Music* tested a long line of nannies before they met their match in Maria. Despite her youthful foibles, she had the outstanding trait of a professionally trained nanny—the ability to both nurture and educate her young charges. In contemporary America, Baron von Trapp would find it far more difficult to be provided with a steady stream of qualified applicants. Though the nanny business is booming stateside, there are more families who need trained nannies than there are available nannies. Interestingly enough, in today's nanny market it's pretty safe to say that a girl like Maria would not have been placed in the baron's home. Most nanny schools would consider the baron's strict attitudes toward discipline, and Maria's technique of gentle persuasion an unsatisfactory match.

As popular as nannies were in Europe, for many years the nanny was an alien concept to middle-class Americans. The word itself didn't fit comfortably into the vernacular; it was the province of the very wealthy and it connoted a veddy British accent. Franklin Roosevelt and Winston Churchill both had beloved nannies, but for your average folk there was simply no need.

But now that attitude has changed, and so have "nannies." The live-in child care business has rapidly become a highly diversified and specialized field. Just the decision to hire someone to care for your child on a live-in basis raises a host of questions. What's the best type of caretaker for my family? Do I want someone trained in child care in this country, and what type of training does the American nanny receive? Does the British nanny have an edge over her American counterpart? Would my family be just as happy with a caretaker who has no professional training? Is a mother's helper all I need? What are the differences in the expectations that I would have of an American nanny, a British nanny, or a mother's helper?

A professional nanny, British or American, is usually a graduate of a formal child care training program. A mother's helper, on the other hand, doesn't have formal training, but if she's young she generally has baby-sitting or a related type of experience. Older mother's helpers tend to be women who have raised children of their own but also lack formal child care training.

THE AMERICAN NANNY

In this country, there are two types of training that qualify someone to call herself a professionally trained nanny. The college-educated nanny (a fairly rare breed) is usually between twenty-one and twenty-five years of age and has a degree in child psychology, child development, elementary school education, or pediatric nursing. She's usually a recent graduate and has not yet found work in her chosen career, or she is taking a sabbatical from teaching or some other child-related profession. In most cases she has had substantial hands-on, paid and volunteer experience with children and is interested in working as a nanny for a year or so before she decides on a permanent career goal.

More common is the graduate of one of the many nanny schools that have opened in this country in the last few years. This nanny's training is more specific than the nanny with a college degree, and she will probably be looking at her career as a nanny with a more long-term perspective. Leaders in the nanny school industry hope that by providing professional, specialized training they can raise the status of the nanny to a more respected level. Be aware, however, that standards at these schools are anything but standardized.

Trained nannies can earn double the money of day-care workers. These women have deliberately chosen this career or left other professions, such as teaching, accounting, and secretarial work. They find nanny work stimulating and like the prospect of travel to another part of the country that often accompanies it.

If you're hiring a professionally trained nanny, she should have a number of specialized skills related to babies and young children—bottle sterilization, children's hygiene, toilet-training theories, organizing children's play, and childproofing a home. It's also a good idea for her to have practical health care skills, such as training in swimming and water safety, first aid, and nutrition.

Ideally, the professionally trained nanny should have a basic understanding of child psychology, but mothers with nannies have told us that this varies a great deal according to the experience, training, and personality of the nanny. A nanny taking care of a preschooler should be able to instruct the child in some form of arts and crafts, have storytelling ability, and should know how to introduce the child to the world of books. For a school-age child, a nanny sometimes has to act as a school liaison, help the child with homework, and sometimes attend PTA meetings and parent-teacher conferences. Again, these skills and responsibilities vary highly from nanny to nanny.

Tuitions for nanny schools differ over a wide range, depending on the length and intensity of the training. Development Center for Nannies in Arizona, a state-accredited program, charges a five-hundred-dollar tuition for in-state residents and seven hundred dollars for out-of-state residents. The course consists of 130 hours of training —40 hours in the classroom and 90 hours of at-home course work. On the more expensive side of the spectrum is Midway College in Kentucky which charges thirty-five hundred dollars per year for a two-year course. The first class will graduate in May 1987.

Some parents are so eager for professional nannies that they arrange to pay their tuition. One family in Iowa had a baby-sitter they liked so much that they sent her to nanny school to improve her skills in areas such as art, music, language arts, and fine motor skills. When a family decides to contribute to, or wholly subsidize, a nanny's education, they usually pay tuition directly to the school.

Some schools are accredited through their state department of education, but nanny schools vary greatly in the

thoroughness of their curriculum, their entrance requirements for applicants, and the criteria required to graduate. Some programs offer college credits and some even
offer associate degrees, while others are no more than a
few dozen hours of classroom work. The level of course
difficulty, the length of the program, and the credentials
of the faculty and administrations are the keys to the
quality of the training.

The American Council of Nanny Schools at Delta College, University Center, Michigan, is a nonprofit coalition
of state-accredited nanny schools. It has established certain guidelines for certification for its member schools, of
which there are fifteen. The core curriculum includes
courses in child growth and development, interpersonal
skills, health and safety, and nutrition. Each school must
have a minimum of two hundred contact hours (lectures,
direct supervision, classroom work, field trips, and discussions) and fifty hours of field experience (supervised, non-
paid work with children). The average school has a fif-
teen-week program during which students attend classes
for five days a week or work in day care centers from eight
to five.

Despite these guidelines, there is still considerable variety even among the certified schools, and American-
trained nannies, unlike their British counterparts, will not
have to take a standardized national certification test until
late 1987. At that time nanny candidates will be tested in
three areas: their general knowledge of child care, their
ability to handle "what if . . ." child care situations; and
by a review of a portfolio of their child care experiences.

While the council has been a leader in establishing standards for the industry, you should be aware that there are
some very good schools that are not members of the council. The National Academy of Nannies, Inc. (NANI) in
Denver, Colorado, opened its doors before there was a
council, and its program is more extensive than that re-

quired for certification. The academy requires 1,043 hours of training over a seven-and-a-half-month period. The first four months are spent in the classroom, the second three actually living in with a family, and the last two weeks back on campus taking a battery of written and oral exams which must be successfully completed (along with a favorable report from the "trial family") in order to graduate.

The Original Nannies Unlimited in Atlanta, Georgia, does not fulfill the council's requirement of two hundred hours of training, but since 95 percent of the nannies it places are already certified elementary school teachers, its director feels that the eighty-hour training program is more than sufficient. Nannies from this school receive some of the highest salaries in the country, about nineteen hundred dollars a month.

Because there's such a large demand for trained nannies, parents have to be especially wary of schools that represent themselves as training grounds designed to provide them with highly experienced help. The fact is, there are currently only about six hundred graduates of certified nanny schools in the United States and a number of programs and students fall well below the minimum standards required to be a trained nanny.

We heard of one program that holds *one-day* seminars on child care and then presents its "graduates" with diplomas certifying their status as trained nannies. One family told us they were paying fifteen hundred dollars a month for a "nanny" who, they discovered, was a graduate of a Saturday workshop. They had taken her certificate at face value and failed to question her credentials (or lack of them). The exasperated mother told us that she arrived home one day to find the nineteen-year-old nanny crying uncontrollably because "she couldn't get my son to finish his chicken salad." The mother continued, "The girl couldn't cope with basic responsibilities, which we chalked up to her getting adjusted to the new situation. We had to let her go after five weeks; she was sincere and affectionate, but totally inexperienced and pretty immature." Needless to say, the next nanny the family hired had to substantiate her credentials much more thoroughly.

How can you avoid costly and time-consuming mistakes such as this? Joy Shelton, the director of the American Council of Nanny Schools has some helpful suggestions for evaluating a nanny school and its graduates.

What are the credentials of the school's director and staff? What is their own specific training and experience? (Don't be afraid to ask direct questions.) Is the school operating legally within the state? Is it licensed? Some schools are not. If the school operates a placement agency, does it have a license for placement? What admission criteria does the school have? Most of the country's nanny schools require applicants to be at least eighteen years old, have a high school diploma, be willing to undergo psychological testing, and allow a criminal record check to be run on them. Graduates of most nanny schools must have a clean bill of health for certification also. Find out how many students, if any, fail to graduate from the program—the national failure rate at nanny schools is 10 percent.

Although it became a federal law in 1986 that those with criminal records could not work with children, some nanny programs are associated with state community colleges that are forbidden by law to run criminal or credit checks on applicants. If they are responsible, however, directors of these nanny programs do point out to applicants that if they have a criminal record, are learning disabled, or have a serious health problem, placement agencies are not likely to find employment for them. Parents should be aware that when searching for a criminal record, some nanny schools check only local police records. Others go statewide, and some do nationwide criminal checking through the FBI. Such checks, incidentally, can be done only with an applicant's permission.

If at all possible, visit a nanny school to see its facilities and meet its faculty and students. Obviously the more you know about a school the better off you'll be when considering hiring one of its graduates. While it would be helpful to speak to parents who've employed nannies from the schools, we were told by several nanny school directors that most parents are reluctant to give out their names to prospective families because they don't want their privacy disturbed. So don't count on speaking to "satisfied customers" when you're evaluating the schools.

Most schools teach a generalized approach to the issues of child rearing, discipline, and sex education, and they instruct the nanny to follow the parents' beliefs in these areas. A good nanny school or placement agency will take a complete profile of both students and families and try to match them according to their needs, skills, and ideas about child rearing.

The director of a nanny school should explore whether the prospective nanny and family have similar philosophies of child rearing. Will the nanny be able to consistently deliver the kind of discipline the family wants? Will a nonsmoking nanny be able to live in a houseful of smokers? If a family is very neat, can it tolerate a more casual nanny? One nanny told us how difficult it was for her to adjust to a mother who wanted every article of clothing put away on hangers—buttoned up. What about allergies? An allergic nanny could have a problem in a house with pets. These kinds of profiles are even more important when the matching process is being handled long distance without an opportunity for the nanny and family to meet in person. The guidelines provided for working with private employment agencies provided in Chapter Four will help you work with a nanny school placement agency as well.

Students at most nanny schools in the country are supposed to learn a wide range of psychological skills, from dealing with a pass made by the husband to handling the mother's jealousy over the nanny's relationship with the children. The students' assertiveness training classes are designed to help her with job management problems, such as resisting the tendency a family might have to overburden her with longer hours or extra chores.

But what if a nanny is unhappy with a family or vice versa? The director of the American Nanny Council suggests that communication can help prevent this. "We encourage nannies and families to sit down and talk with one another at length every three weeks, especially during the first six months they are together." They should be very open about their list of expectations: Are they being met? If not, why not? If communication gets muddy, the family or nanny can call the school for intervention. Policies in this area vary, but if the relationship breaks off and it is agreed that the nanny is "at fault," there is usually some sort of refund or replacement policy. Generally this applies only during the first thirty to ninety days of employment, so be sure to ask specifics.

One mother told us about the first nanny she hired. She admits that experience taught her to be more direct in her questions about child rearing because she and her nanny could never agree on her daughter's bedtime. "As far as Jill [the nanny] was concerned, it was eight o'clock, no earlier, no later. But there were times when I wanted to play with Karen, especially if I got home late from work, but Jill disapproved of any departure from the schedule. I know she meant well, but it just didn't work out, so now I have Eileen, who's more relaxed and flexible."

The major function of the nanny is to provide care,

warmth, and security in the absence of the parents, to prepare healthy meals for the child, to plan activities that stimulate the child's desire to learn, to teach the child appropriate manners, etiquette, and dress, and to carry out the parents' wishes for discipline.

Though every professionally trained nanny should have basic training in child care, what's expected of her in terms of specific responsibilities will differ from family to family. Generally, a trained nanny is not expected to do anything around the house more than light housework. Depending on the individual nanny and the additional salary arrangements, specific duties other than child care can be tailored by an agreement between the nanny and her prospective employers.

Additional responsibilities beyond the parameters of a trained nanny's expected duties should be negotiated before the signing of a contract. These include various levels of cleaning, errands, laundry and ironing, grocery shopping, cooking, and entertaining.

Most of today's professionally trained nannies come from middle-class families and can be devastated by feeling that they are being put in the category of a servant. A Scarsdale nanny told us that the nanny schools didn't prepare their students for the loneliness they encountered. One young Pittsburgh nanny complained that she felt uncomfortable in the baby park. She said that when mothers discovered she was a nanny, not another mother, they shut her out. Still another nanny had to deal with her own mother's negative reaction. The mother, who had her M.A. and was getting her doctorate, couldn't understand why her daughter wanted to be, as she put it, "an overpaid domestic." Because these seemingly minor matters can sometimes become major problems for the nanny or the parents, try to be aware of the undertones of your relationship with your nanny by keeping the lines of communication open. How responsive the parties are to the sensibilities of each other can determine the success or failure of the relationship.

BRITISH NANNIES

Almost without exception a British nanny has longer and more comprehensive training overshadowing that of her American counterpart. All British trained nannies must take a two-year course at local colleges or at specialized nanny schools, after which they test for the Nursery Nurse Examination Board (NNEB) Certificate, for national certification. The curriculum consists of courses in growth and development of children, physical development and keeping children healthy, cognitive development and learning through play, emotional development, social relationships, and rights and responsibilities of the children, the family, and the nursery nurse in employment. And because of their standardized, high level of training the requirements of British nanny schools serve as models for some American schools.

The Norland Nursery Training College in Berkshire, England, is one of three private accredited nanny colleges (the other two are Princess Christian College and Chiltern Nursery Training College). Its program is worth mentioning for any parents considering a British nanny. (Norland's prestige and appeal are transatlantic, but most of its graduates [most British nannies, in fact] are working illegally in the United States. For information on the legalities of hiring a foreign nanny, see Chapter Five.)

Norland was founded in 1892 by Mrs. Walter Ward, who held the philosophy that educated women should care for children in their early life, and that these women should be provided with specialized training. Today, Norland has minimum academic entrance requirements, but no entrance exam. Norland students are eighteen or over when they begin their training and at least twenty when they assume their first jobs. The students complete their two-year training in a large Georgian mansion situated in a park of a hundred and fifty acres, complete with tennis courts and an outdoor swimming pool. The registration and tuition fee at Norland comes to the equivalent of three thousand U.S. dollars. Louise Davis, the principal of Norland, told us that the school accepts seventy-six students each year.

Norland nannies are required not only to have had hands-on experience at local nurseries and primary schools, but also to have spent one term getting practical experience at a hospital. To be awarded the Norland Primary Certificate, the student must have passed the College Assessment and the NNEB examination, and she must have completed twelve weeks of hospital training in maternity and sick children's wards. Norland students then begin their careers as probationary nurses. After nine months of successful work experience (favorable reports from employers), they receive the full Norland diploma and badge. The minimum salary for a probationary nurse is the equivalent of seventy-five U.S. dollars weekly, plus room and board. In the United Kingdom, the qualified Norland nurse earns the equivalent of $150 to $300 per week, plus room and board, but the director of the Fox Agency in New York City told us that she has clients "willing to pay anything" to get a Norland nanny who can work here legally. To acquaint American students with Norland Nursery Training, Midway College in Kentucky is working to develop a six-month exchange program with the British nanny school, but it is not yet in operation.

UNTRAINED HELPERS
AND MOTHER'S HELPERS

Almost everyone we interviewed agreed that the most important characteristics of a live-in helper are intelligence, sincerity, and affection toward children. These qualities cannot be learned at a nanny school, and a number of mothers gave solid reasons for preferring untrained helpers over graduates of a formalized child care program.

Generally, the untrained helper has no specialized training beyond a high school education. She may be a girl between the ages of eighteen and twenty, just out of high school, or a woman newly arrived in the country with little or no English. She may also be an older woman whose children are grown or who wants to switch careers as she heads for retirement. One mother couldn't praise her fifty-eight-year-old mother's helper enough. "She's patient and kind—nothing seems to ruffle her, and I don't have to be looking over her shoulder to check on her. She *knows* kids because she brought up three of her own."

This independence of the older mother's helper, coupled with her stability, was a desirable trait mentioned by a number of mothers. Unlike the eager young helpers, the older women needed little, if any, supervision.

The younger mother's helper usually costs less to employ and brings a high level of energy and enthusiasm to her work, but it's important to remember that, just as the term implies, a *mother's helper* needs a *mother* available, which means that a young mother's helper is really just a second pair of hands. These girls always need some sort of adult supervision. As much as mothers valued their mother's helpers, over and over they told us, "It is like having an older niece living with us."

The untrained helper that most mothers look for has certain basic qualities—the desire to be with and care for young children, the ability to set up realistic expectations for them, a pleasant disposition, the ability to manage the daily routines of the household, the adaptability to deal with an emergency should one arise, and, of course, dependability.

The untrained helper will usually provide child care and a wider range of household chores—cleaning, grocery shopping, errands, and meal preparation—than will her trained counterpart. But all these expectations should be defined and negotiated at the beginning of the employment arrangement.

Interestingly enough, we spoke to quite a few mothers who shared the feeling that, in spite of the fact that they do need close supervision, an untrained helper's lack of formal child care was an asset. The fact that professionally trained nannies look at child rearing from a structured point of view presented a problem to some parents. Those same parents mentioned that hiring an untrained helper lessened the chances of conflicts over imposing their own child-rearing attitudes against the theories of an "expert" nanny. There were others, however, who, in retrospect, would have been willing to pay more for a helper who required less "mothering."

Because of the scarcity of professionally trained nannies and the many employer applicants per graduate, some families we spoke with hired an untrained helper and then provided her with on-the-job training and course work. They took advantage of many community resources, such as public libraries and local colleges. The Red Cross and the local YMCA also offer many courses in child-related subjects and the tuition for these classes is generally quite reasonable. A sample of courses you might wish your helper to take are: first aid, CPR, swimming, child development, nutrition for children, creative activities for children, child care workshops, and family health.

HIRING A MOTHER'S HELPER FOR THE SUMMER

Most summer helpers are between the ages of fourteen and twenty-one. They too are essentially just an extra pair

of hands, and because they are working in the summer—
often at resorts or vacation homes—they sometimes have
a tendency to think that they're also on vacation. We
talked to a few mothers who tried to circumvent this
problem by hiring "townies," local high school girls, but
this did not turn out to be a very good approach. They
reported that familiarity with their surroundings made
these girls even more likely to be distracted from their
responsibilities.

It's a better idea to bring your local summer helper with
you on vacation, and build in prearranged time off. This is
important for two reasons: it's necessary and fair to your
summer helper and it reinforces the idea that time off is
time away from regular responsibilities. Time off implies
time on.

Pay varies widely for summer helpers—anywhere from
fifty to a hundred and seventy-five dollars per week—and,
as long as the employer makes it clear beforehand, most
are willing to accept a great deal of household responsibilities. Because older summer helpers are able to take on
more duties—driving and housekeeping—they usually
command the highest salaries.

Much of the trouble with mother's helpers comes from
overburdening them with unexpected tasks. A number of
high school summer helpers reported to us that many
parents who would not have imposed so heavily on older
helpers heaped many extra chores on them. When your
young helper first comes to work for you, give her a written sheet listing all the duties the two of you have agreed
upon. Sit down with a pencil and paper and jot down
everything you want her to know about the care of the
children and the running of the household.

One mother's experience with two different mother's
helpers in the course of a single summer illustrates how a
little bit of good luck can turn a fiasco into a triumph.

The family, who vacationed regularly at a summer

home in a beach resort, was about to give up on the idea of summer help. The first girl the mother hired thought she was obliged to provide the entire family with earsplitting entertainment from a radio in her upstairs room. Besides being snide and arrogant, the girl's all-night vigils around town worried the mother no end. A few weeks into the summer, the concerned mother shipped the girl home. When another high school girl was recommended, the mother was just about fed up with the whole idea but reluctantly decided to give it another try. The girl turned out to be a charmingly bright math and science whiz who was looking for a way to make some extra money for college in the fall. Though she was a bit eccentric in her dress, she was extraordinarily affectionate with the children, cooked well, played the guitar, and got a giggling delight out of being a surrogate mother for the rest of the summer.

Understanding the background and training of the type of live-in helper you select will be an enormous asset in establishing a good arrangement. Remember: Well-defined expectations—both yours and your employee's—is the key to success with anyone you hire, from the teen-aged summer help to the professionally trained British nanny. Once you know what your needs are and the sort of person who can best fulfill them, you can begin the process of finding her.

Four

Finding Your Nanny or Mother's Helper

There are basically two ways to go about finding a nanny or mother's helper. The first is through employment agencies or the placement offices of nanny schools. The second involves going it "on your own" by advertising in local or out-of-town papers, or using the tried-and-true technique of word of mouth. Both methods can be successful; each has advantages and disadvantages. Whichever you choose, the following information will help ensure that your experience is smooth and successful.

EMPLOYMENT AGENCIES
AND PLACEMENT SERVICES

A number of mothers we talked to swear by employment agencies and nanny school placement services. They feel that an agency saves them time and frustration by providing qualified applicants and by acting as middlemen if problems come up after the live-in helper has been placed. Others feel that agencies are an expensive waste of time, that the women they've hired through agencies haven't worked out any better than others they've hired on their own.

Our sense is that a good agency can be an enormous help, but that you do pay a price for it. The person you hire through an agency will command a higher salary (a minimum of $125 a week), is likely to expect benefits such as medical insurance, and will probably have to be paid "on the books." You will also have to pay a fee to the agency. Some mothers we talked to wanted to use agencies but just didn't feel they could afford it. You will have to decide if you want to absorb these extra costs. If you do, find an agency that is worth it.

As with nanny schools, there is an enormous range of child-care-related employment agencies. Some have been in business for decades—Gallagher's in Wellesley, Massachusetts, has been placing nannies and domestics for fifty years—while others have been in operation only a short time. Some are large, placing hundreds of workers a year, while others are basically run by one person or, in some cases, are part-time businesses. The level of training of the candidates supplied varies, as do the methods of recruiting and interviewing those candidates.

An agency is only as good as its last placement, and the best recommendation you can get for an agency is a referral from a friend who has used it. But even with such a referral (and especially if you're just beginning to look for an agency) there are still some questions you should ask the director before you put yourself in her hands. Use the list of questions in this chapter as a guide, and remember as you talk to the various agencies to trust your own instincts. We found that there were some agency people we liked and some we didn't, and we could tell in the first few minutes of conversation. If you don't feel comfortable with the representative you're talking to—you find her too authoritative, too unorganized, too snobbish, or whatever—ask to speak to the director or manager. If you're still uneasy, call another agency.

SOME GOOD QUESTIONS TO ASK THE AGENCY OR NANNY SCHOOL PLACEMENT DIRECTOR

1. Where do you get your applicants?

Find out if they are local candidates or ones who have been recruited from out of town. If the agency places non-U.S. citizens, ask if these women have their green cards. Does the agency use newspaper advertising? Does it recruit from local colleges or high schools? Does it get referrals from other women it has placed? Ask if you can be given the names and phone numbers of some of its clients. An agency that gets referrals from both the applicants and the clients is obviously doing something right.

2. What level of experience do your applicants have?

If you're looking for an older woman with years of experience, or a professional nanny, don't waste your time going to see an agency that only places young women from the Midwest. Find out exactly what types of live-in helpers it supplies. Weston's Domestic Employment Agency in Los Angeles, for example, can probably find you a real British nanny complete with green card, but it also handles the more typical (and sought after) house-keeper/child care worker. Nannies Unlimited in Duluth, Minnesota, does place young candidates from the Midwest. All are carefully screened; many have several years' experience.

3. What is the salary range that your applicants expect?

Asking this simple question in advance can save you a lot of time. If the candidates are getting $250 a week and up, and you can't pay more than $150, you need to find another agency.

4. What is your fee?

All employment agencies charge a fee, payable by you, the client; this is how they make their money. But policies differ. Some agencies charge a flat fee, ranging from a low of $400 to a high of $900. Others base the fee on the salary. The charge may vary from the equivalent of two weeks' or one month's salary or 10 percent of a year's salary. In some cases you will be asked to pay a retainer fee, which will be applied to the placement fee once a nanny is hired. If you do not hire one of the agency's candidates, however, the retainer fee will probably not be refunded.

5. How do you select the applicants you represent?

You have standards and you want the agency you're dealing with to have some too. The Helping Hands Agency in Connecticut, for example, requires that all applicants be at least eighteen, have a high school diploma, be able to swim, have a valid driver's license with a clean driving record, and have at least three child-related references. The agencies that came most highly recommended to us and the ones that we felt best about told us that they turned away more applicants than they represented. The usual figure was one applicant accepted out of every three or four.

6. Do you personally interview the applicants?

This may sound self-evident but it's not. There are a number of agencies that recruit young women from out of state but never meet them in person. They do, of course, check references and interview them by phone, but you may not feel very comfortable with this procedure.

Some of the agencies that follow this practice have been very successful with their placements and enjoy very good reputations. You'll have to decide if it's more important to you to be face to face with the agency director or to work over the phone with an out-of-state agency director who has met the applicants personally. There is no easy answer to this question. As you might expect, the agencies who interview the girls in person feel that it's very important to do so. They say, and rightly so, that you can learn things about people by sitting down in the same room with them for a couple of hours that you might not discover by mail or over the telephone.

7. Is your agency licensed?

Many states require that, for the protection of the consumer, employment agencies be licensed by the state department of labor. Getting a license normally requires the payment of a fee—about $150—per year; the filing of some paperwork, including such items as references and submission of all forms and documents that will be used to conduct business; the purchase of a surety bond; and, in some states, fulfilling certain physical requirements for office space. This last requirement can be difficult for operators of small businesses and those just starting out. In New York State, for example, a home office cannot be licensed unless the owner is disabled. In Connecticut the office must consist of at least two rooms and have a separate entrance.

If an agency that interests you is not licensed (and we

talked to some directors of unlicensed agencies who were as thorough and intelligent as their licensed colleagues), ask it why. You may find that its reasons are satisfactory to you.

Regardless of whether the agency is licensed, there is one more thing you can do to assure yourself that you are dealing with a reputable business. Call your local Better Business Bureau or Consumer Affairs Department to find out if there have been any reports on an agency that you are considering. If you find that there have been a number or pattern of complaints or any serious charges, you're obviously going to look for another agency.

8. Is the agency bonded?

If an agency is licensed, it probably had to put up a surety bond that would be forfeited if it was shown that it had not fulfilled its obligations properly. In some cases the applicants will be bonded as well.

You might also ask if the agency does a criminal check on its applicants, and whether such a check is made through the local police or through the FBI. One agency in Minnesota that conducts an FBI check found that one of its candidates had recently been released from an Illinois prison, where she had been serving time for child molestation. Some agencies will run such a check only if you request it, so it's certainly worth asking about.

9. Will you replace a nanny who "doesn't work out"?

Again, policies differ. The best guarantee we heard about was from Versatile Care in Atlanta, Georgia. They will replace the nanny or mother's helper any time within the first four months. The director feels that it takes this long to really be able to tell how things are working out. We found a thirty-day guarantee to be more typical, however, and you should not work with an agency that doesn't at least offer that.

Remember, though, if the woman you've hired leaves for "cause," you won't get a nickel back or another placement from most agencies. "Cause" might be something as serious as physical abuse, but it might also be something as seemingly simple as asking the woman to do more work than you originally agreed to. That's why agencies recommend, and many require, a written agreement specifying duties, wages, and method of payment.

What Happens Once I've Picked an Agency?

The better agencies are as concerned about the well-being and happiness of their applicants as they are about the families with whom they place helpers. A number of agencies said they began their businesses to counteract the "slave trade" that had developed. Don't be offended if you are asked a lot of questions. A good director will want to know what kind of living conditions you can offer, how many children you have, what your daily routine is, and what your expectations for housekeeping are; she may even ask for personal references for you. All these questions will help the agency director make a better decision in referring candidates to you.

Versatile Care in Atlanta is one of the most sophisticated agencies in this regard. A member of its staff meets with the entire family in its own home before sending a single applicant to be interviewed. The agency insists on meeting the entire family because it wants to be sure that the husband and wife are consistent in their expectations; it has found that disagreements between the spouses lead to unhappy placements. It has also found that by meeting the children it can get a clearer sense of the family's needs. The family must also outline both verbally and in writing just what the duties of the nanny or mother's helper are expected to be. Versatile Care's application form asks such specific questions as how many times a week an employer wants the house vacuumed and the laundry done. Other questions posed by the representative from the agency range from the basic—Do you want a young woman, or a more experienced one?—to some that are more subtle—Are you looking for someone to become a part of your family or do you want a more professional relationship?

Most agencies don't go to quite such lengths, but be wary of an agency that doesn't ask at least some of these questions. After all, you are paying for its ability to make a successful match, and that will be more difficult to do if it doesn't have some sense of your lifestyle and your expectations. Some agencies even administer the Minnesota Multiphasic Personality Test—which poses such questions as, "Would you rather spend an evening watching television, reading a book, or going to a party?"—to its applicants, and sometimes to the families in order to improve the chance that the family and the applicant will get along. Without exception, every agency director, parent, nanny, and mother's helper told us that a good placement is to a large degree a matter of matching personalities.

Once they know what you're looking for, agencies will probably send you résumés and perhaps pictures of a number of possible candidates. Some, like Versatile Care, may even provide videotapes. From these résumés you may select several candidates to interview. We'll talk about the interview process later in this chapter.

ADVERTISING

Newspaper advertising is a much less expensive way to find potential nannies and mother's helpers. You will most likely have to do a lot of preliminary screening to weed out the obviously unqualified, but you will probably come up with at least three or four candidates who are worth interviewing at length. City and town dailies and weeklies were most often mentioned, but we did hear of families who had good luck placing ads in college newspapers and on bulletin boards.

Though there is some crossover, parents we talked to fell into two groups: those who advertised in their local papers and those who advertised out of state. Those who chose to advertise locally said they did so because they wanted to be able to interview the women in person, and (for some parents this was the more important reason) they felt that "it would be much less hassle." These families didn't want to worry about a potentially homesick nanny and they didn't want to absorb the cost of the airfare if things didn't work out.

Out-of-state advertising is becoming increasingly popular, however. Most of the ads are concentrated in newspapers in just a few regions: the upper Midwest, the mountain states, and, to a lesser degree, northern New England.

The upper Midwest appears to be the most consistent supplier of mother's helpers and nannies, and the Minneapolis *Star Tribune* was mentioned most frequently as the best way to reach these young women. The Sunday edition of that paper reaches a five-state area, including Minnesota, North and South Dakota, Iowa, and western Wisconsin.

A number of mothers we talked to mentioned a "Mormon connection" ("they don't drink and they don't smoke") as particularly appealing. A representative from the Salt Lake City *Tribune* confirmed that they run "hundreds of ads a month," but she also told us that for a few years the Mormon Church discouraged girls from replying to out-of-state ads. That reaction came in response to the girls' reports that they were being exploited by their employers, and to allusions (although no charges were ever brought up) of some kind of prostitution ring. Parents became understandably reluctant to send off their daughters.

In the last year, however, the Church has removed some of its restrictions; the *Deseret News*, a Church publication, now accepts out-of-state domestic advertising again, and the area may once again be a good source. It's interesting to note that the Salt Lake City *Tribune* runs a warning, advising girls who are responding to out-of-state ads to get very specific information about the nature of the employment. You should also know that you can't specify in your ad that you are seeking a Mormon, that not everyone who responds to your ad will necessarily be a Mormon, and that, as one woman put it, "some of those young Mormons are just looking to leave home so they *can* smoke and drink."

PLACING YOUR AD

A call to the classified department of the paper of your choice is the first step. The representative can give you the rates, deadlines, and method of payment. In some cases you might even be able to place your ad over the telephone.

Rates are based on a per line charge, usually about twenty-five characters or five words to a line, and there is generally a three-line minimum. There is often a different rate for out-of-state ads—the Minneapolis *Star Tribune*, for example, charges $5.90 a line in state and $11.00 for out of state—so be sure to specify. Most people we talked to placed their ads in the Sunday edition.

Some newspapers have several different Sunday editions and these have different deadlines. The Milwaukee *Journal* and the Minneapolis *Star Tribune* have both a metropolitan edition and a statewide or multistate edition. The deadline for the latter is always a day or two earlier; specify that you want the widest circulation possible, and wait for the next week if you've already missed the deadline for that issue. It's worth the delay to get the fuller coverage.

You'll get more responses if you place your ad in the early spring when high school and college graduates are beginning to think about "next year." So if you can possibly manage it, place your ad at that time.

WRITING THE AD

The best advice is to be specific. If you are looking for someone young, say so. If you want a nonsmoker, state it. If you are looking for someone with several years' paid experience, make that clear. There's no guarantee that this will weed out all the unqualified applicants, but it's a start.

Specify the number and general ages—infant, toddler, and so forth—of your children. The candidates have a right to know that you've got two-year-old twins or three children under three before they respond. State your family situation: single mother, single father; "professional couple" seems to be the lingo for a two-career family.

Describe the living conditions: "own room and bath" or whatever. If the helper will have to share a room with the child, say so up front. If you're advertising locally and you live in a particularly nice area, mention it. If you are advertising out of state, remember that the name of your suburb will probably mean nothing. Washington, D.C., area is better than Chevy Chase, Maryland; suburban New York means more than Westchester County.

If you have amenities, you should mention them. "Family pool," "use of the country club," or "weekends at beach" may prove very attractive. If she'll have personal use of a car, say so.

People seem to be split about whether you should mention a specific salary. Clearly, if you are offering a high salary, list it. Be sure and mention benefits like insurance.

Specify that you expect references.

You will need to decide whether you want to receive responses by phone or by mail. If you're advertising locally, the phone is the obvious choice. If you are advertising out of state, the decision is a little tougher. All the classified advertising representatives and most of the parents we talked to said that you will get more responses if you give your phone number. The reasoning was that many of these young women are responding to a number of ads, and they don't want to write seven or eight letters.

If you are giving your phone number, be sure to specify the best time to call. If you are listing a home number, and you're at the office all day, you'll get nowhere unless you say, "Call evenings." You should also say to call collect. Don't count on an answering machine to take messages since many people are still intimidated by machines. If you can't plan to be home, hire an answering service to pick up your phone. Have them answer, "Muney residence" (or whatever) rather than "service," and have them take the message.

You may prefer to get an application in writing first. If you are uncomfortable about listing your address (which takes up space), consider getting a post office box for a few weeks, or arrange with the classified department of the newspaper to have responses sent there. Ask for a picture, but do not ask for a résumé unless you have already specified that you are looking for a person with experience. If you're looking for a young woman just out of high school, simply ask for a letter describing herself and her experience. From what people have told us, that's what you'll get anyway, and you may scare off some good candidates who just don't know how to put together a résumé.

WORD OF MOUTH

Whatever other method you use in your search for your live-in helper, you ought to be using word of mouth as well. It's as useful in this situation as it is when you're trying to find a job for yourself. Let people know you're looking.

Talk to friends and acquaintances both with and without children. Tell relatives. Go to the parks and playgrounds; other mother's helpers and nannies are often a great source. We talked to many mothers who got a nanny because she was a friend or relative of someone else's nanny. The nanny network is a very strong and well-connected one.

PRELIMINARY SCREENING OF APPLICANTS

If you are interviewing through an agency or nanny school the preliminary screening will have already taken place. If you are not using an agency, here are some tips to help you.

Your first telephone conversation doesn't need to be lengthy. Ask the applicant a few questions about her previous jobs, how long she worked at them, why she left them. In the case of a younger candidate ask her about her family, schooling, and experience with children. If she's from out of town, ask her about her reasons for leaving. Clarify some of the statements you made in your ad, or if this is a word-of-mouth candidate, describe the job. You should be able to tell quickly whether or not the person warrants further consideration. If the person sounds promising you might ask her at that point to send you a letter or résumé and references, or you might simply say that you'd like to talk further in a day or two.

Many women who've hired young nannies from out of state recommend talking to the parents as well. You can get a better sense of the candidate's upbringing and another view of her experiences. You can also ask them if they feel she might get lonely or homesick.

If your initial contact is by letter or résumé, think about how much you can reasonably expect. If you're looking for a professional, you have a right to expect a résumé that has been put together professionally. If you're not, scale down your expectations. Most parents who had advertised successfully told us that they weren't necessarily looking for beautifully written, insightful letters. They were looking for neatly written letters that indicated that the people writing them genuinely liked children and wanted to work.

Once you've narrowed down the field of candidates, you are ready for a more in-depth interview. Some aspects of the discussion that follow pertain specifically to interviews in person, but much of it is applicable to telephone interviewing as well. A final word of advice: if you are going to handle the interview long distance, ask the candidate to send a recent photograph.

THE PERSONAL INTERVIEW

If at all possible, have the entire family meet with the applicant for part of the interview. Don't just assume that whomever you decide on will be fine with your husband or wife, even if he or she tells you just that. We've heard of too many cases where conflicts over the choice of the live-in helper arose later; usually punctuated with the line, "I could have told you she was lazy/dishonest/rigid after five minutes with her; how could you hire her?" This is also important for your potential nanny's protection; she should feel comfortable with both of you as well.

See how the applicant responds to your child, but keep

in mind that a certain level of tentativeness will be natural on the part of both. Explain to your child (if he or she is old enough) that this is someone who might come and live with you and help take care of him or her. Some mothers suggested letting the child show the applicant his or her room as a way of their getting to know each other. After the applicant leaves, ask your child what he or she thinks. If he or she expresses a negative opinion, listen. If your child says he doesn't like her, but you do, perhaps you can arrange for another visit in a few days. But if after a second try, your child still has a negative attitude, don't hire her, even if you think she's terrific. You can't fight a child's gut instinct, any more than you can fight your own. Keep looking.

If your child is an infant, let the candidate hold him, perhaps even change a diaper or give a bottle. You want to be sure she feels comfortable with babies. She could be terrific with a toddler, but not so wonderful with a three-month-old.

Watch her body language, but again keep in mind that some nervousness is to be expected, especially if she is just out of school. Is she fidgety? Does she meet your eyes when she talks to you? Is she well mannered? Is she neat?

As you interview the applicant, start with simple questions she can answer easily without much thought. This should put her at ease. Ask about previous jobs, her high school or college, what she studied, what her activities were. Ask about her family, brothers, and sisters.

It is important to get some sense of how your potential live-in helper feels about discipline. We talked with both nannies and mothers who split company over this issue. In one case the nanny had worked well when the child was an infant, but the mother felt that she wasn't flexible or patient enough when the child was asserting some two-year-old independence. In another situation the nanny felt that the parents were inconsistent with their discipline and that it undercut her own authority.

Some mothers we talked to recommended asking very direct questions in order to get a sense of the applicant's child-rearing and disciplinary philosophies. While this can be useful with an older applicant, our sense is that a younger woman may not have formed or be able to articulate her child-rearing philosophy yet, and that direct questions may be difficult for her to answer. Remember, too, that asking hypothetical questions—"What would you do if my child . . . ?"—can sometimes backfire. The applicant often tries to figure out what response you want and that's the one she gives.

A better approach is to ask her how she was brought up. Were her parents very strict? Were they tough disciplinarians? Did she have curfews? Ask her how she feels about it; does she think she'd do things differently? This will give you a better clue as to what her predispositions toward child raising are.

You might also ask her how she handled certain situations when she was baby-sitting (or on previous nanny jobs). Did any of the children she sat for have temper tantrums? Fights with siblings? Did she ever sit for a colicky infant? What did she do when she couldn't get a child to take a nap? Ask what kinds of activities she enjoyed most on her baby-sitting jobs. Who were her favorite families or children to sit for and why? Asking specific questions that she can answer from experience are better than asking hypothetical ones. Some parents also recommend describing your own methods of discipline, and then just asking if the applicant agrees with or could at least go along with it.

Ask if she has any children, and, if so, how they are and what they are doing now. We talked to one mother who, when interviewing long-distance, took the woman's statement that she "had a daughter" to mean that she had experience with children. The mother was floored when the woman arrived from Maine with her fifteen-year-old daughter in tow.

The following list should be used as a guide to conducting the interview. Not all will be applicable to your own situation, but do take time to conduct a thorough interview. It is startling how many nannies told us they weren't asked many questions at all. And be sure to allow her the opportunity to ask you questions as well.

To Get Things Started

Describe yourself and your family and your routines. Tell her why you want live-in help. Thoroughly detail the job, hours, accommodations, days off, vacations, overtime policy, salary, and benefits.

Describe your child or children. Their relationships to one another and to you and your spouse. Their strong personal traits—shy, outgoing, competitive, temperamental, physically active, creative, and so forth—and how these qualities manifest themselves. Any "phases" they are currently in—"Daddy's girl," he wants to dress himself, the terrible twos, and so on.

Suggested Questions

- Why do you want to be a nanny?
- Do you see child care as a career?
- Do you have any children? How old? What are they doing now?
- Have you ever been away from home before? For how long and under what circumstances? How do you feel about leaving home? Do you think you might get homesick?
- Tell me about your previous jobs. What did you like and

not like about them? Why did you leave them? How long did you work there?

- Tell me about your experiences with young children. What was the worst experience you ever had baby-sitting? What did you enjoy most? What kinds of things did you like to do with the children you sat for? Who were your favorite families? Why?
- Tell me about your family. Do you have brothers and sisters? What are they doing now? Are you the youngest, oldest, or in the middle? What was your family routine like? Do both your parents work? Were your parents very strict with you? If you did something wrong, how were you punished? Do you think you'll do things differently with your own children or bring them up in pretty much the same way?
- Tell me about your high school or college. What were your favorite subjects? What activities were you involved in?
- Are you a licensed driver? For how long? Have you ever gotten a speeding ticket or other moving violation?
- Can you swim? Do you have any Red Cross swimming certification? Would you feel comfortable supervising children in the water?
- Do you have any experience taking care of pets? Do you have any allergies to animals? Would you mind helping to take care of our pet(s)?
- Do you smoke? Will it bother you if we do?
- Do you drink? Will it bother you if we do?
- Have you ever used any drugs?
- Have you ever been arrested?
- Are you religious? Do you attend religious services? Will it bother you if we are/are not religious?
- Can you cook? With help? Are you willing to learn? Would you cook for the children? For the family? Can you grocery shop? Do you have any food allergies? Do

you have any special diet needs? or, Would you mind adapting to our special diet needs?
- Have you had a physical examination in the last year? May we see the results? (Many agencies require this; you might want to as well.)
- What do you like to do in your free time?
- Whom can we call as references, and how do you know them? (The agency should provide these.)

CHECKING REFERENCES

You should insist on a minimum of two child-related references. Ask the references how long and under what circumstances your applicant worked for them. Ask them how much she was paid, and what her duties were. What did they like best about her? How did the children like her? What was the biggest problem they had with her?

If there are inconsistencies between what she told you and what they tell you, ask about these differences. Remember that most people are going to be leery of giving too damaging a "review." They may feel partially to blame if a situation didn't work out. Because of this, one mother told us that the best question you can ask a reference is, "Would you hire her again?" Her previous nanny had given her as a reference, and not one of the prospective employers asked that simple question. Her answer, by the way, would have been no.

It's important to find out if the person given as a reference had the same needs and expectations that you do. She may tell you how terrific a particular person was, but unless you know some specifics about their household, that information may not mean much. A mother in Chicago told us that she had to fire a nanny who had gotten raves from her previous employer, who, it turns out, had wanted someone to "take charge" of the household and the child. This mother, on the other hand, found the nanny too set in her ways and they both found the situation impossible.

MAKING THE DECISION TO HIRE

The person you hire to live with your family and care for your children must be someone you can treat with both respect and affection. And every member of your family needs to feel that way about her. When we asked mothers what advice they would give another mother about to hire a nanny, they consistently said, "Trust your instincts." To that we add, "Hire someone you like."

Once you've made the offer, go over the specifics again. Discuss any house rules that you feel are appropriate, such as telephone and visitor privileges, and curfews. We can't urge strongly enough that you put this information into a written contract which you both sign. Many agencies require this and will use it to iron out potential disputes. See Chapter Seven for detailed information on this. The clearer you are up front, the fewer problems you'll have along the way.

Five

Au Pairs and Foreign Workers

For generations, an easy way for many foreign women to enter the United States was by the au pair route. In exchange for room, board, and a round-trip ticket, a young woman from abroad would live with a family for one or two years, caring for the children and perhaps doing the housework as well. After a year or two, the woman would leave, usually to return to her home country, she having had a chance to experience living abroad, the host family having gotten domestic help at relatively low cost.

Many families prefer hiring help from overseas for reasons other than saving money. It is an opportunity for the children and parents to come in close contact with a different culture and unfamiliar customs, and to learn a smattering or more of another language. There is the allure of the exotic to consider as well: Someone from Marseille is, for many, more attractive than a person from Mankato. And so the search for the perfect au pair—one who will clean the house, teach the children French, and happily cook three-star meals—continues.

In 1973 labor department and immigration regulations complicated this search. The U.S. Immigration Service tightened its regulations, essentially eliminating the "nonpreference" visa that au pairs had long used to enter the United States. It is now much more difficult than it used to be to hire a foreign domestic worker. However, it is possible, though time-consuming and laborious, to follow the legal route. And, though we don't recommend them, there are less than legal ways of obtaining foreign help.

We'll go into greater detail about all of the methods that people use, but the basic ones are:

- Petitioning the government to bring someone from abroad.
- Helping a worker, already in the United States, to obtain a "green card" or permanent legal status.
- Employing someone already in the United States to work for you who doesn't have a green card.
- Hiring someone through either of the two new "au pair" cultural exchange programs.
- "Importing" a worker on a tourist visa specifically to work for you.

HOW THE LEGAL PROCESS WORKS

Only about 270,000 permanent resident immigrant visas are issued each year, with a maximum of 20,000 from any one country. Permanent resident immigrant visas are only for those who want to reside permanently in the United States, that is, for those who wish to work or live here. There are no quotas on visitor's visas, which do not carry with them the right to work. A green card is the immigration visa that allows a foreigner to live and work legally in the United States.

There are six preference classes of immigration visas. Domestic workers come in under the lowest, or sixth, preference class: the one for skilled and unskilled labor in short supply. Only 10 percent of all immigrant visas can be issued to people in this sixth class, or about twenty-seven thousand domestic and other workers per year. If you are trying to bring in a nanny from overseas, she will get no special treatment and be lumped in with this group.

Getting green-card status for a foreign worker will not be easy. In addition to the competition for a relatively small number of places, you will face a complicated application procedure. (A Canadian family wishing to hire a nanny from overseas must follow a similar procedure, though a Canadian immigration official told us that approvals for live-in domestic jobs are generally rubber-stamped.)

You must start by proving that there is no U.S. citizen or legal resident in your area whom you can hire to do the job. Since sixth-preference visas are issued only to workers "in short supply," it will be up to you to prove that your sitter isn't taking a job away from a qualified unemployed citizen. The procedure, a standardized one, is known as *job certification,* and it's handled by the labor certification board of your state employment office.

Job certification begins when you fill out form ETA 750. Part A of this form asks you to describe what your nanny's living conditions will be, the size of your family, and the job specifications. You must guarantee that you will provide free a private room and board. In addition, you are asked to describe the efforts you have made to find someone locally to fill this job, but don't worry about it if you haven't made any at this stage. There will be time for that later.

Part B of ETA 750 asks for information about the qualifications of the person you want to hire. In order to demonstrate that this person's qualifications warrant bringing in a noncitizen to do the job, you have to show that your nanny has at least one year of paid experience in her field. This is defined as 2,080 hours of work (full- or part-time). This means you or the worker will have to give dates, hours worked, wages paid, at least one notarized letter from a former employer, and other data to support your claim. You must also submit a copy of your contract with this future worker, specifying her or his job description, including hours, wages, and duties.

Once you've filled out ETA 750, it goes to your state employment office. At this point you are required to run an ad for the position in a newspaper of general circulation for three consecutive business days. If you haven't already done so, you are also required to file a job order with the state employment office, to run for at least thirty days. If either of these methods produces any qualified candidates for your job, you must interview them—and you'll have to have a valid reason for rejecting them in favor of the foreign-born worker. Remember, what seems like a legitimate reason to you may not seem so to labor department officials. As you consider candidates to live in your home and care for your children, reasons like "I just don't trust her" or "My kids didn't get along with her" may seem to you to be more than adequate. To the labor certification officer considering your application, these reasons won't suffice. You'll need more specific objections. Some that are considered acceptable are that the job applicant didn't show up for the appointment, was clearly unreliable, had no or unsatisfactory references, was unreasonably late for the appointment, or smelled of alcohol.

You must also agree to pay your area's prevailing wages for domestic work, so that it's clear that your choice of foreign help isn't based on undercutting local salaries. Your state employment office will have established the minimum prevailing wage for your area. This will be at least equal to the current federal hourly minimum wage.

After your job has been listed with the state employment office for thirty days, the job certification application is sent to the regional certification office. There are ten of these nationwide. They make the final decision about whether or not to certify the job you are offering; that is, to agree that it warrants issuing a labor certification, which in turn allows the alien worker to apply for an immigrant visa. This decision, and a copy of your ETA 750 form, will be sent to you as the employer, or to your immigration lawyer.

Once the job has been certified, you face a second process, this time one run by the Immigration and Naturalization Service (INS). You must send your ETA 750 form and an I-140 form petition to the INS, which will validate its *priority date*, the date on which it was first filed with the labor department. In addition, you will have to prove that you can afford to pay the salary of the worker. INS then sends your form on to the embassy of the alien's origin, where the form will be processed according to the priority date.

As you can see, the process of legally certifying a job and then obtaining a green card is a difficult and uncertain one. Just certifying a job can take anywhere from three months to a year, with the longer period of time more usual. And in most parts of the country certification is extremely difficult to obtain at all. We were told by immigration attorneys that the New York metropolitan area is the only region where live-in domestic jobs are routinely certified, if documentarily qualified. Even if your position is certified, it will still be a few years before your chosen nanny can enter the country. The State Department is currently processing sixth-preference visas with priority dates of two years ago. Visas for Mexican and Filipino immigrants are even more backed up.

GETTING YOUR JOB CERTIFIED

There are two good reasons why you should try to get yourself certified as an employer who needs foreign-born help. One is that the certification allows you legally to bring over an immigrant from abroad. The other is that it permits you to help an immigrant currently living here to get a green card so that he or she can remain in the United States and legally work for you. Although certification is a difficult and lengthy process, there are some things you can do to improve your chances at it.

You should know that in order to get certified as an employer of live-in help, you must prove it a "business necessity" (that is, the business of running your household) that you have such help. Day help usually can't be certified because the Immigration Service does not consider that day workers are in short supply. Having only one working parent does not qualify as a business necessity in most areas, although it can if the nonworking spouse can show a busy schedule—volunteer work, travel, attending school, and so forth. If you are part of a two-parent working couple, you may still need to be creative in demonstrating your need for live-in child care. Some people argue that live-in help is a business necessity because they frequently entertain in the evenings for business reasons. Others point out that both partners must work lots of overtime, that both parents travel, or that the two parents work split shift. If a member of your household is a doctor on call, or belongs to another profession in which he or she is unexpectedly called away, you might have a better chance at demonstrating the need for a round-the-clock child care worker.

One woman was advised by her immigration lawyer to make the job description sound so miserable and drudging that no one in her right mind would find it desirable under any circumstances. She advertised for someone who would be willing to care for her children, prepare and serve all meals, clean the house, and do laundry for the entire family. The prospective employer was also resourceful enough to run the ad in the least popular paper in town. Labor certification was satisfied because it was a paper of general circulation; it just happened that very few people read it.

Parents interested in hiring foreign nannies may be especially drawn to the chance for their children to learn another language. But you can't use "French-speaking" or "Spanish-speaking" on your job description as a way of ruling out local applicants for your live-in job. The whole justification for allowing noncitizens into the United States to work is that no citizens are being thrown out of work by the immigrants. That's why every aspect of the job you are trying to get certified has to be justified as a *business* necessity, not just a matter of personal preference or convenience. If you can show a business reason why you need a baby-sitter who speaks another language —for example, that you frequently travel on business to French- or Spanish-speaking countries and must take your children with you—then you can justify language skills as a qualification for a nanny. But in the eyes of the Labor Department, simply wanting your children to be bilingual does not justify hiring an alien rather than a citizen.

HELPING AN ILLEGAL OR UNDOCUMENTED ALIEN TO GET A GREEN CARD

Although it is illegal for a noncitizen to work without a green card, it is not currently illegal for you to *hire* someone without a green card. And if you have someone working for you who is seeking permanent legal status, it may be in your interest to *sponsor* that person—to help him or her get a green card. It's true that once an immigrant has permanent legal status, he or she may be interested in finding work other than child care. But in order for status to be granted, the immigrant must continue to work for you while the application process is going on. Since it takes about two to three years to get a green card, you are in effect trading your sponsorship for several years of guaranteed service.

Sponsoring an immigrant can be a long and costly process. Most people hire an immigration lawyer, which can cost as much as twenty-five hundred dollars over the three-year period. This cost is sometimes borne entirely by the person seeking employment here, or it is shared with the sponsor. It's a negotiable factor in the process.

In order for someone to be sponsored, he or she must have at least a year of experience as a domestic with you or be able to provide documentation for a year's work elsewhere. At the end of the year, you simply begin the process of certification, including advertising for local job applicants and listing your job with the state employment service. Although your immigrant worker will have had at least a year's experience, you can't require more than three months' experience from the U.S. applicants.

One danger of applying for job certification for an immigrant who is working illegally is that the immigrant might be deported. This is a very tricky situation and new regulations have made it even more so.

First of all, remember that job certification and applying for a green card are actually two separate processes. Job certification is handled by your state employment office, while the actual issuing of the green card is handled by the INS. It's true that if the INS finds out that an immigrant is working without a green card, it will probably try to deport her. But since job certification isn't handled by the INS, that agency has no way of knowing about the immigrant until she actually applies for her green card, after the job certification has come through. Remember too that once a job has been approved for certification, there is still a several-month wait for that job's priority date to come up. Until recently a skilled immigration lawyer (or you) could time the application to the INS for a green card to coincide with the priority date coming due. Now, however, you must file with the INS within sixty days of certification. Though this puts the illegal worker in a kind of immigration limbo—her job is certified, but she still has a wait to get her green card—most lawyers believe that at this time deportation is unlikely. You should know, though, that at the end of this process your worker must return to her home country so that the final paperwork can be processed by the U.S. embassy there.

AU PAIRS

If you are applying for a job to be certified, don't use the term "au pair" on any of your forms. Au pairs are not considered workers "in short supply," and hiring an au pair won't be seen as a justifiable alternative to hiring a U.S. citizen. In addition, most au pairs don't want permanent resident status in the United States (as a matter of fact, most stay here for only one year) and so won't qualify

for immigrant visas, which are only for people who want
to live here permanently.

LEGAL AU PAIR PROGRAMS

Happily, there are some recently instituted programs
under which au pairs are allowed to come into the country legally and work for U.S. families for a limited period
of time. In 1986 the United States Information Agency
authorized two pilot programs that place young British
and English-speaking Europeans, between the ages of
eighteen and twenty-four, with American host families
for one year. Each au pair lives in an American home as a
family member who is available to assist with child care.
The Au Pair in America Program, sponsored by the American Institute for Foreign Study (AIFS) Foundation, intends to place six hundred au pairs in its first year. The
AuPair*Homestay USA, under the auspices of the Experiment in International Living, intends to place five hundred. Each program expects to bring a thousand au pairs
in the second year. To better provide a support system for
these young women and host families, the au pairs will be
clustered in major metropolitan areas.

AuPair*Homestay USA is operating in the New York
and Washington, D.C., areas during its first year, with a
third region to be added the second year of the program.
Au Pair in America is also focusing on these two areas but
is sending au pairs to Boston, Denver, San Francisco, Atlanta, Philadelphia, and Chicago as well. Both programs
provide community counselors as a resource for the au
pairs and families.

These au pairs shouldn't be considered full-time employees or housekeepers, since a primary thrust of the
program is cultural exchange. The director of the Experiment program reminded us in fact that the term "au pair"
means "on par with," a definition that has been lost in

translation. The au pairs will enter this country on J-1 "cultural exchange" visas that are valid for one year. Fees for these programs include travel, pocket money, medical insurance, counseling services, social activities, an orientation program, and cultural events for the au pair.

Both programs are being closely monitored by a U.S. government interagency review panel. At the end of the two-year pilot plan, a decision will be made whether or not to extend and expand the programs.

Qualifications of Au Pairs

Prospective candidates are screened through the London office of the American Institute for Foreign Study, or by Experiment officers in England, Denmark, Switzerland, and West Germany. Besides the age requirements (eighteen to twenty-four), au pairs must have a secondary school diploma or certificate. They may have completed some college or may have a diploma in child care. They must also be fluent in English. While many AIFS candidates are from Great Britain, others come from Scandinavia, Holland, Germany, Ireland, Austria, Switzerland, France, Italy, or Spain. Au pairs from the Experiment program come only from those four countries where the Experiment has offices.

All candidates must be in good health and are required to undergo a medical checkup to ensure this status. They must also have a valid international driver's license, unless the host family specifies that this is unnecessary. It is a given that the au pair must enjoy working with young children and have prior child care experience such as baby-sitting or looking after younger siblings. Both programs require that the au pair follow the Code of Conduct which forbids use of illegal drugs, excessive use of alcohol, rudeness, or discourtesy to host families. The code also requires au pairs to inform host families of any travel plans for time off well in advance.

How the Program Works

Prospective host families submit applications to the AIFS or to the Experiment in International Living. They are then interviewed in their homes by the field staff of the foundation. Once a family is approved, the matching process is begun, and here the two programs differ. AIFS families are given the applications of up to three au pairs with whom the AIFS encourages phone interviews (at the expense of the host family). The host family then informs the foundation of its choice and the runners-up go back into the pool of au pairs still seeking matches. In the Experiment program, the families are not given a choice of applicants. The match is made by the office at the end of the interview process. At that point, however, they do encourage the host family to contact their prospective au pair by telephone.

Though guarantee and refund policies differ, the directors of the two programs told us that every effort will be made to replace an au pair should it be necessary. If, of course, it is determined that the problem lies with the host family, no replacement or refund will be made. These situations will be dealt with on a case-by-case basis.

It takes approximately three months to process applications and au pairs arrive only in June, September, or January, so a host family should apply by April 1 for a June arrival, June 1 for September arrival, and October 1 for January arrival.

Both programs encourage families who have successfully participated to reapply for the following year. Though they will, of course, have a different au pair, "repeat" families will be given substantial discounts.

Responsibilities of Host Families

Host families must provide au pairs with a private room and include her whenever possible in family meals, outings, holidays, and other events. Au pairs must also be given the opportunity to attend courses for four to six hours a week at a local adult education program for the purpose of cultural or personal enrichment.

The host family agrees to give the au pair one complete weekend off each month and two weeks off (with pocket money) during the exchange year. The AIFS suggests that this two-week vacation be scheduled at the end of the twelve-month assignment, while the Experiment insists that the vacation take place in the first ten months.

Responsibilities of Au Pairs

The au pair agrees to assist the host family with child care for up to forty-five hours a week. This includes looking after, feeding, bathing, and playing with the child(ren) of the household as well as being present in the home while the child(ren) sleep if a parent is not at home. The au pair must also be home while the child(ren) are absent from school due to illness or school holiday and, if needed, must drive the child(ren) to and from school, appointments, outings, or errands.

The au pair is expected to help the host family with light housekeeping such as preparing meals for the child(ren), helping the parent or older child(ren) maintain the child(ren)'s belongings, making beds, doing some of the child(ren)'s laundry, and straightening the child(ren)'s room(s). The au pair is responsible for keeping his or her room tidy and clean and doing his or her own laundry.

While the au pair's responsibilities do not include heavy housework or running the entire household in the absence of the parents, he or she can be left with the child(ren) overnight on an occasional basis.

Costs of the Programs

The fee for both programs is almost identical and works out to about a hundred and fifty dollars per week over the year. The program fee covers:

- Processing of and interviewing the host family.
- Recruitment, screening, and selection of the au pair.
- Visa application and completion.
- Round-trip transatlantic transportation for the au pair.
- Medical insurance.
- Orientation program for the au pair.
- Pocket money for the au pair (a hundred dollars per week paid directly to her).

HIRING "ILLEGAL" AU PAIRS

Of course, many families hire au pairs who come into the United States on tourist or student visas. These girls are usually found by word of mouth, either through friends or associates abroad or through friends here who have an au pair who has a friend back home. Some families have also had luck placing advertisements in overseas newspapers.

Au pairs "come cheap," as one parent put it, and for many families this is their main advantage. The families we spoke to paid from sixty to a hundred dollars a week, with seventy-five a week about average. Most also prepaid round-trip airfare. You should be aware though that few of these girls stay longer than a year, and many don't fulfill even their year's "commitment." Some families really enjoy having a young foreign girl in their home for nine months or a year, and when one leaves they hire another. Others resent the fact that they go to great lengths and expense to fly the girls over and then they leave before fulfilling the agreed-upon term. To counteract this problem, these parents recommend that the au pair buy her own ticket, to be reimbursed by you when she has fulfilled her year's commitment. If you try this tactic, keep in mind that not all young women can afford such an up-front expense, and you may therefore be reducing your pool of applicants. Later in this chapter we'll discuss some of the precautions you can take to lessen the likelihood that the girl you hire will leave prematurely.

The Legalities of Hiring an "Illegal" Au Pair

It is not illegal for you to hire someone who is in this country on a student or tourist visa, but it is illegal for that person to work. If the worker is caught, she or he will be deported.

It *is* illegal, however, for you to *arrange* for someone to come to the United States on such a visa with the express purpose of working for you. Such an act is considered a conspiracy to defraud the government and is punishable by a two-thousand-dollar fine or five years in prison. It is extremely difficult, however, to prove a conspiracy of this kind, and prosecuting such crimes is a low priority at the INS. As a matter of fact, *no one* we spoke to—prospective employers, immigration lawyers, even employees at the INS—expressed fear that anyone was actually going to be prosecuted by the federal government for bringing an au pair in on a visitor's visa.

Two bills currently before Congress, however, *would* make it illegal to hire someone on a tourist visa, but the status of these bills is uncertain, both in Congress and at the INS. The Simpson bill, which passed the Senate in 1985, and the Rodino bill, which is currently before the · House Judiciary Committee, would both levy strict fines against those who employed foreign workers without green cards. Many observers are skeptical about either of the bills passing; others point out that even if such hiring does become illegal, it's extremely unlikely that the INS will have sufficient funds to investigate and prosecute families employing foreign helpers. As one immigration lawyer put it, you can't legalize jaywalking in New York City, but it's rare that someone is arrested for doing it. In the meantime, countless families continue to import illegal au pairs, and while we can't recommend the practice, we can tell you how they go about it.

Getting an Au Pair into the United States

When a prospective au pair prepares to come to the United States, she files an application for a nonimmigrant visa with the American embassy in her own country. Visitors' visas can be granted for any length of time, with one year being the usual period. These visas can then be extended by six-month increments. Embassies are becoming more aware of the way these visas are used, however, and they are growing somewhat stricter in granting them to women who seem like possible au pairs or nannies. Such women may find it difficult to get their six-month extensions, or even to get full-year visas in the first place. They must convince the embassy representatives that they are legitimate "tourists."

One resourceful Irish girl who had been denied a visa when she applied by mail wore an "engagement" ring when she applied in person at the American embassy in Dublin. She felt the ring was a signal that she had strong reasons to return to her native country. Other girls claim their prospective employers are relatives, while others name a profession they plan to pursue back in their home country. A word of caution about mentioning a profession —a Danish girl who said she was a farmer underwent extensive interrogation about dairy cows at Kennedy Airport. Fortunately she had taken some agricultural courses so she was conversant about her "profession." Your au pair must be knowledgeable about her supposed "profession" before setting foot here, lest the INS send her back home to pursue it immediately.

Once a visa is granted, it is stamped onto the passport, but that is not the end of the paperwork. The prospective visitor also receives a second document, the I-94 arrival/departure record. This form is given to nonimmigrant aliens entering the United States while the rest of us are filling out customs declaration forms. The record of the visitor's arrival is kept by the INS, with the departure part of the form stapled into her passport. The INS will collect her departure form when she leaves.

Simply having the correct visa, however, doesn't guarantee that your au pair or nanny will actually make it through customs. Just as embassies are becoming suspicious about the misuse of visitors' visas, so is the INS on the lookout for au pair or nanny types arriving at the airports. It's not uncommon for zealous immigration officials to pull au pair girls aside for searching and questioning—an intimidating experience for an eighteen-year-old in a strange country.

A Filipino nanny told us about a fresh-faced Scottish girl who was ahead of her in line at Kennedy Airport. The young Scottish girl had a Westchester address as her final destination in the United States. When asked if the suburban residents were relatives, she innocently replied no and was immediately escorted to an anteroom—and probably sent straight back to Scotland.

Those who want to bring foreign workers to the United States usually help their au pairs prepare for the "airport experience." They advise their au pairs or nannies to bring traveler's checks from the home country, so that it looks like they have enough money to "visit" the United States without needing a job. Since it is illegal for you to have paid your au pair's way over, you should not have sent her any personal checks. Nor should her airline tickets be issued on your credit card or through a domestic

travel agency. Families who have faced this problem recommend wiring money via the overseas travel agency
that is handling her tickets or through friends or other
contacts.

A prospective au pair will seem less suspicious if she's
carrying a round-trip ticket with an actual return date,
rather than an open-ended return. Of course, the reserva-
tion can be canceled later. One parent recommended
that the au pair travel with a package tour arranged by an
agency in her home country. A word of caution, however.
Some tours have penalties for cancellations, so refund
policies should be checked.

If the au pair is heading for a city that seems an unlikely
tourist destination, her domestic connection should not
be listed on her overseas ticket. She'll have an easier time
getting through customs with a separate domestic ticket
waiting for her at an airlines counter inside the airport. Of
course, if she's claiming her employer as a relative or
friend of the family, this last subterfuge is probably unnecessary.

Should the au pair face questioning, she'll most likely be
asked about her tourist plans, so she should have an itiner-
ary of people to visit with names and addresses. Many
parents give their au pairs names of their friends to list.
One mother sent her expected au pair a letter (signed by a
friend) to carry with her that detailed "travel plans" they
had made for her. If the woman's prospective employer is
mentioned, she should make it clear that she's a friend of
the family. Naturally, if you are picking her up at the
airport, you should not bring your kids! If your address is
identifiably an upper-income neighborhood, particularly
in New York City, an au pair might get through customs
more easily if she gives another address as her first destination, or if she puts down the name of a New York hotel.

Since an au pair may be searched, she should not carry
any incriminating evidence with her. Everyone inter-

viewed warned against au pairs arriving with "change of season" clothing. Those clothes can be sent later. Photo albums or framed pictures from home might also serve as a clue to immigration officers that the au pair is planning a long and settled stay; like seasonal clothing, photographs can always be sent on afterward.

Likewise, an au pair girl should be careful not to carry any correspondence that might suggest that she's coming to the United States to work. A letter from her prospective employer, or a note from a friend back home, might refer to her new job. If an immigration officer sees it, the au pair will get shipped right back to her homeland.

Making it through immigration once is no guarantee of immunity from scrutiny, especially when returning to the United States after a short visit abroad. Two Belgian girls went home for Christmas and returned after a two-week stay. The immigration officers at the Dallas–Fort Worth Airport (though we had heard that the airport was an easy one to slip through, this story convinced us otherwise) were immediately suspicious of the girls' status when they saw from their passports that they'd only been gone a short while.

The officials grilled the girls about their legal status, searched their luggage, found pictures of children and a diary in Dutch which the INS people immediately had translated into English. The diary detailed the daily activities of one of the au pairs with her host family, a revelation that infuriated the officials. They told the terrified teenagers that there was a plane leaving for Belgium in ten minutes, that they had to be on it, and that they had to sign a paper stating they were willing to leave the United States.

Luckily for the girls, an employee of another airline intervened and offered to "make sure the girls got on the plane back home." Away from the INS officers, he told the girls that they had been the victims of harassment because they hadn't been advised of their right to see a lawyer. He delayed the girls long enough that they missed the flight to Belgium, but the INS officers weren't finished. They took the girls *under guard* to a nearby hotel and it was only some very smooth talking by their then-frantic employers and their lawyers that got them released.

The lesson here is to impress upon your au pairs *not* to carry *anything* that identifies their status in the United States. Although the girls *were* being harassed, it was careless of them to be carrying pictures of the children they took care of and, worse, to have a diary in *any* language that described their day-to-day lives as au pairs. We also heard about another girl who was deported upon the discovery of her Scarsdale library card. You just can't be too careful.

Once an au pair has made it into the country and has worked here for some time, the question of extending her visa comes up. Immigration lawyers generally agree that if someone wants to apply for a green card, it's a mistake to try to extend a visitor's visa. The extension application will have to include a false statement affirming that the tourist hasn't been working, while the sponsoring family applying for job certification will have to claim that the tourist has been working. If the tourist does not apply for a green card, it's extremely unlikely that anyone would check her extension application for false statements. With the green card effort, however, she invites investigation. And while it is a civil offense to overstay one's visa, it's a criminal offense to lie on an extension application.

Although it is technically illegal to overstay a visa, it's unlikely that a tourist who did so would ever be caught unless she got into some other kind of legal trouble. A tourist who is caught is subject to deportation, but not to any other type of penalty. Generally Immigration does not deport overstayed tourists but allows them to leave with a "voluntary departure" order.

What worries most au pairs about overstaying a visitor's visa is the fear that they won't be able to get another visa once they leave the United States and then want to return. Again, there is a discrepancy between what is technically legal and what the INS and the State Department have the power to enforce. Many lawyers believe that the embassies just don't have the record-keeping procedures to keep track of whether an applicant for a visa ever overstayed a previous visa. If the former au pair "loses" her passport with the old visa and gets a new one, this procedure is even more difficult.

A few stories we heard bear out the wisdom of this advice. One Swedish girl working in San Diego felt guilty about overstaying her tourist visa, so she applied for an extension. By the time the INS got around to informing her that her request had been denied, she had long since returned home—seven months after applying for the extension. Another immigration lawyer applied for a tourist visa extension on behalf of a client only to be told that the INS couldn't find the *original* I-94 arrival form in order to issue an extension!

Yet another lawyer is convinced that all immigration departure forms are stocked in cartons at Kennedy Airport, never to be seen again by anyone, anytime, anywhere. Some people simply advise losing the departure form and not filling out another one, so that no record will remain of your departure date. While this is actually not legal, a departing tourist is unlikely to attract the attention of the INS.

FINDING AND SCREENING AU PAIRS ABROAD

Newspaper advertising is often a fertile source for finding foreign women and men who want to do live-in child care. But be careful! Even if you are advertising in a respectable publication, you have no way of knowing what kind of a response you'll get. Make sure you have some way of checking the references of your prospective au pair, and that you have reasonable assurances that she or he can be trusted with your child. You might consider requiring a photograph to help give you a sense of who is answering your ad.

One couple we interviewed requested a mature person with experience in child care. Their ad specified a non-smoker and requested a photograph. They got one picture of a woman posed in a cabaret with a drink in one hand and a cigarette in the other! They also heard from a computer student who plainly admitted that he wanted the job in order to better his career chances by learning English.

The *International Herald Tribune* was recommended as a good source of nanny and au pair ads. About twenty-five such ads per week are placed through the paper's New York office. The *Tribune* is considered reliable because it attracts a more sophisticated group of applicants seeking work in the child care field. The kind of young woman who is aware of the classifieds in the *Tribune* is probably a little more savvy than the average young girl looking for work overseas.

If you are traveling overseas or have friends abroad, you should check the classified sections of local papers. You (or a friend on your behalf) can not only place ads in these publications, you can also find listings for domestic agencies who can find au pairs for you.

The Irish Echo, a U.S.-published newspaper, is a highly thought-of source of ads for Irish live-in helpers already in this country. They run about sixty ads per week, primarily "help wanted" with some "situations wanted" as well. As hiring foreign helpers becomes more popular, the *Irish Echo's* advertising in this area is increasing. Many people who found au pairs through the *Echo* are referring their friends to this useful publication.

Locating the right live-in helper depends, in part, on your own resourcefulness. Get to know the au pairs in your own neighborhood: one of them may have a friend who's dying to work in the United States. Also, make use of any personal or professional contacts you have overseas. One American mother found her French au pair because the girl's mother was a neighbor of some family friends of the Americans.

Of course, all the resourcefulness and screening in the world can't prevent mistakes. The following story illustrates that, in some ways, you can never do enough screening and interviewing.

A couple in Denver had friends in New Zealand who placed an ad in the appropriate local paper and even did preliminary screening for their friends back in the United States. After screening final candidates for the job, the Denver couple selected a woman whom they had interviewed by phone. They cabled eighteen hundred dollars to a travel agency in New Zealand to cover the young woman's airfare.

She arrived and was welcomed with open arms by her host family. In short order, however, the parents realized that, in spite of all their precautions, they were faced with a disastrous situation. They learned that the young woman was dragging their ten-month-old all over town on her personal errands. They discovered that she was incredibly sloppy—the mother found herself constantly doing the girl's dishes and laundry—and exceptionally lazy. She habitually slept late and one afternoon the mother returned home to find her baby crying while the girl napped. As it turned out, one of the reasons for her fatigue was that she had arrived pregnant! In spite of all this, the family was reluctant to fire her because they had made a personal and financial investment in her. Nevertheless, the girl was so totally unacceptable (she even asked the family to pay for an abortion) they had to let her go after only five weeks. Having tried so hard to find the right person and having searched so far for her, they felt particularly betrayed and vowed never to hire foreign help again.

HELPING YOUR FOREIGN WORKER TO FEEL AT HOME

When you hire a live-in worker, you're not simply entering an employer-employee relationship. You're taking a stranger into your home to care for your children and become part of your family. If the person you hire is unhappy, your whole family will feel it, particularly your children. It's very important to be sensitive to the needs of your live-in helper or au pair and to help her adjust to the strains of living with a new family in a foreign country.

Loneliness and homesickness are the two biggest problems your au pair (and thus you) is likely to face. We can't stress this enough since these factors were mentioned by almost every family and au pair we interviewed. This is true of anyone who leaves her friends and families behind, but even more true of those who live, not among their countrypeople, but in the homes of "foreigners." This problem is compounded if the person adjusting is a teenager who has never left home before. And if your au pair is from a country that is very culturally different from this one, she will face even greater stress in learning how to handle living here. In some ways, taking in an au pair is almost like being the host family of an exchange student. You face the responsibility of helping to bridge the cultural gap, a responsibility that can be draining and time-consuming.

Before you hire someone from another country, check to see whether anyone else of that nationality is living in your area. Will your au pair or live-in helper have the chance to meet a network of people from her home country? If not, she may feel isolated and depressed, which will certainly affect your own home life. The most successful placements we heard about were those where there were three or four girls from one country who could act as a support group for one another. The Experiment and AIFS au pair programs recognize this and make a point of clustering their placements. You should do the same.

Scout your neighborhood or area for other au pairs of the same nationality. Introduce your au pair to an existing play group that has other au pairs (not mothers—their problems are different). You might also encourage your au pair to enroll in an adult education course that might help her meet other people with common interests. It's a way of making her feel part of the community, giving her some sense of belonging.

MISCELLANEOUS CONCERNS

RELIGION

Religion is a sensitive area that must be considered when you're hiring foreign help from countries where religion and culture are closely intertwined.

One couple in Indianapolis received four letters from Irish girls who seemed promising. Two of them mentioned that they were "strong practicing Catholics," which was fine with the mother of the family. The father, however, felt that he, not the au pair, should have sole responsibility for his child's religious upbringing. He felt that a self-professed, strongly religious person would unduly influence his child.

Another au pair we heard about was miserable because she and her American family didn't share the same religious background. She felt so isolated being Catholic in a Jewish home that she returned to Ireland.

We strongly suggest that you ask a prospective employee if the family's religion makes a difference to her.

DRIVER'S LICENSE

Check the existence and/or status of your au pair's driver's license—whether it is full or provisional—before her arrival. Any valid license from a foreign country is valid here in the United States for at least one year. After that time is up she should investigate getting a U.S. license.

If an au pair has a provisional license, she has only the equivalent of a learner's permit in the United States. In Ireland, for example, you can get a provisional license when you're eighteen; these are then renewable for up to three years. Many Irish girls under twenty-one don't have a full license; they simply renew their provisionals. Your Irish au pair might tell you she drives (and she does) but her license will not be valid here. It was six weeks before one New Jersey family discovered that their Irish au pair's license was no good.

It is possible for your au pair to get a U.S. license—all she needs is a valid passport. But check with your local department of motor vehicles to see if your state also requires a social security number. If it is required, apply as soon as possible for a *nonworking social security number,* since these take about four or five weeks to obtain.

LANGUAGE CONSIDERATION

You should think about the level of English competency you'll be comfortable with. Some families have no problems communicating with an au pair whose English is not that good or heavily accented, but this might drive others crazy.

When you hire someone directly from overseas, remember that even five years of high school English is no guarantee of fluency, and that letters and telephone conversations are not necessarily accurate measures of fluency either. At the very least, make sure you talk to the person on the telephone.

We found that many parents who had hired "light" English-speaking help were amazed at how well the au pair and the young children communicated; the mothers commented that the children and the girls had evolved their own language, much like immigrant children do, moving smoothly from one language on the street to another at home. A few mothers, however, expressed concern over what might happen in a real emergency. Others simply said that they found the language problem tiring.

If your child is still an infant or just learning to talk, there is still another consideration, and that is language development. One family who had had a French au pair for a year was warned by its pediatrician not to hire the Polish girl it was considering for the next. The doctor was concerned that the succession of *different* languages would be a problem for the child who was just beginning to talk, and he felt it would be better to hire another French-speaking au pair. At the very least, he suggested, the au pair should be asked not to speak Polish to the child.

Hiring an au pair from overseas can be a rich and rewarding experience, and it can result in a close and warm relationship that will last a lifetime. A number of families we talked with keep in touch with girls who worked for them years ago and have visited them in their home countries. And the girls have returned here, not to work but to legitimately travel and stay in their homes as guests and friends. One au pair, now mature and married, named her

new baby after the little girl she cared for in St. Louis, so
the relationship could be one of an extended family.

But every precaution should be taken to assure both
you and the girl that the time she spends in your house
will be as enjoyable and pleasant as possible for everyone.
Make sure you don't take any shortcuts, or think there is a
quick and easy way of hiring someone. Minimize the sur-
prises; discuss any topics or areas that might be a possible
problem with you, your spouse, your older children, and
of course the au pair. And keep your fingers crossed. It is
an important step and one that can be a delightful and
loving time for you and your child(ren).

Six

Living with Live-In Help

Anytime people live or work together, problems are bound to come up. If people are both living *and* working together, the situation can be even more volatile. If you've followed our advice so far, though, you are ahead of the game. You and your live-in helper have a clear sense of your expectations for child care and housework, her living arrangements, salary, and time off. You've thought through the relationship and anticipated some of your family's possible reactions to this new member of your household.

But no matter how carefully you've screened your live-in helper, you are still going to have to face some adjustments when she becomes a part of your household. If you think back to all the living and working situations you've been a part of, you'll realize that this is inevitable. You may love your job, your boss, your roommate, or spouse, but there are still times when the situation can get a bit rocky. As many women put it, "I adore my husband, but sometimes he just drives me crazy."

BEFORE YOUR LIVE-IN HELPER ARRIVES

Don't forget that your child is the most important person in this situation. If your child is old enough, it is crucial that you discuss with him or her the helper's coming before she actually arrives. You may have done this during the interviewing process, but a child's memory is short. One mother told us that she and her daughter had had a long talk about Lucy before she was hired, but when she arrived three weeks later the four-year-old had completely forgotten about her. In the intervening time between hiring and arriving, take as many opportunities as possible to talk about the live-in helper who is coming. Your child can help prepare her room, or the two of you can make a list of things to show her when she arrives. If your live-in helper is from another part of the country (or from out of the country), point out her hometown on a map.

Explain to your child that someone is coming to live with you to help take care of him or her, and to help with some of the other work around the house. Your child should be helped to understand that this person will love and take care of him or her, and that she will be in charge when you are not around. If you are going back to work for the first time, take your child to your office and, if he or she is old enough, leave the phone number there at home so that your child understands where you are each day. As one mother commented, "I think I made a mistake when we first hired a nanny for Daniel. I didn't really take the time to tell him why someone was coming in and I think it was very confusing for him. He didn't know why I was gone so much, and he didn't know how he was supposed to relate to this new person."

PREPARING THE LIVE-IN HELPER'S ROOM

A key to maintaining a certain level of privacy for your family and for her is to make sure your live-in helper is comfortable in her room. She needs plenty of closet and drawer space, a comfortable bed, a nightstand or table, good light, and at least one chair; a desk is a useful extra, if you can provide it. She should also have some way to control the room temperature. This last requirement may not seem worth mentioning, but we've heard more than one story about freezing nannies in drafty attics. If you need air-conditioning or heating, she will too; and she certainly ought to be able to control her room temperature by opening and closing a window. If you're creating a room for her in a basement or an attic, make sure that it can be maintained at as comfortable a temperature as is the rest of the house.

Every mother and live-in helper we interviewed stressed the importance of providing the live-in helper with her own television. Buy one if you have to—it's one of the best investments you'll make. A clock radio is also important (and it's inexpensive), and if you have an extra stereo or tape player, so much the better.

All members of your family should understand that the live-in helper's room is strictly off limits unless they are specifically invited in.

THE FIRST WEEK

It will take some time for your live-in helper to get acclimated to her new environment. This is particularly true if she is arriving from overseas or another part of the country. She may need a few days just to get over jet lag or the initial "culture shock." Even if she's coming from across town, it's best not to expect too much the first few days. "I think I had a kind of fantasy," one mother admitted, "that the nanny would arrive, see what needed to be done, and would just take over. I didn't realize how many things I would need to explain."

If at all possible, arrange to take off a few days from work. Give her tours of your house, your neighborhood, the parks, schools, shops, and so forth. Introduce her to neighbors and teachers, and—very important—to other nannies or sitters. Show her how to use the appliances and where supplies are kept. Do not, however, expect her to remember everything.

Plan some activities for the three of you but be sure to give your helper and your child plenty of opportunities to be alone together. She should begin taking over some of the child's care as soon as she's been shown the routine.

Discuss the contract again, and start off on the right foot —remember, it is hard to change patterns once they have been established. If you secretly hope that your new helper will turn out to be Mary Poppins, you may well be in for a disappointment; if you give her a list of specific duties and she turns out to be willing to do much more, you've had a pleasant surprise.

This is also the time for a more in-depth discussion of your child care philosophy. Policies on nap time, feeding, punishment, television, safety rules, manners, and friends should be spelled out. If your daughter doesn't finish her lunch, is it all right for her to have dessert? If the helper has made a grilled cheese sandwich, and your daughter decides she wants a peanut butter one instead, is it all right to give her the peanut butter or is she expected to eat "anything that's put in front of her"? Do you regulate the hours and types of television programs your child watches? Do you feel strongly that she gets a detailed explanation about every prohibition or is it all right with you if the live-in helper simply says, "Because I said so." Do you let your infant "cry it out" or do you want her picked up the instant she cries? Obviously you can't cover every possible situation, but the basics should be discussed at the beginning.

HOW MUCH "OFF-DUTY" TIME SHOULD SHE SPEND WITH US?

The question of the helper's free time came up frequently as we talked to live-in helpers and mothers. You may want her to feel free to join you "after work" to watch television with the family—or you may not, wanting this time for the family to be together. Likewise, she may want to know whether you are inviting her to enjoy a family party or outing, or whether you are expecting her to continue watching the kids or taking care of the housework. As always, be clear about your expectations.

Most live-in helpers do eat with the family and enjoy it, but it's wise to ask yours how she feels about this. We talked to some who would have preferred to eat in their rooms. One helper told us, "My first family wanted me to eat with them and I didn't know how to get out of it. They thought they were doing me a favor. But all it meant was that I worked through dinner as well, keeping an eye on the kids and jumping up to get things from the kitchen. I wouldn't have minded if they had counted it as work time, but they thought they were giving me a break."

Most live-in helpers make their own lunch and breakfast and yours should have access to the kind and amount (within reason) of foods she likes. If there are items in the refrigerator or cupboard that are off limits to her, make that clear.

HOUSEWORK

You will have already outlined your live-in helper's housekeeping responsibilities, but you should go over the details again when she first arrives. And if her main responsibility is taking care of your child, you'll have to figure out how she should balance that with anything else you expect her to do.

Many helpers felt that mothers who had spent at least some time at home alone with their children were much more reasonable in their expectations than those who had not. Remember that your helper isn't a superwoman any more than you are.

Several helpers mentioned a problem of "mixed messages." "She'd tell me that the child came first, but if she came home and the vacuuming wasn't done because we'd had such a good time at the park, she'd be annoyed," reported one. Another told us, "I like the family I work for, but it can be very frustrating. I'm told that I'm on my own, but, somehow, it always turns out I've made the wrong decision."

You will probably find it helpful to sit down at the beginning of each week (or even briefly each morning) to go over the list of chores and other responsibilities. This is the time to say that "the house has to be clean by Thursday because I'm having a dinner party, and I don't care how much Lauren screams." Specify which tasks must get done, and which can be left to her own judgment depending on how things are going with the child.

SPECIAL OCCASIONS

You and your family are going on a long-awaited week's vacation in a cabin by the lake, and you are looking forward to sleeping late, taking it easy, having a chance to unwind. Life will be a lot easier if you have your live-in helper along to do the housework and child care as she does at home. Do you take her with you?

Yes, of course—as long as you understand that it's not *her* vacation but yours, and that you may need to compensate her for the extra work that may be involved. If her joining you means that she gives up her own time off for the week, you should pay her extra for those days. In any case, you should not confuse this time with her vacation. She'll be a better companion for your children if she gets her own time off, away from the family.

Of course, these arrangements should be worked out as far ahead of time as possible. If your live-in helper's job requirements include accompanying your family on business trips and vacations, she should agree to that condition before she's hired. One family we spoke to thought that their au pair would be thrilled at the chance to spend a couple of weeks with them at Aspen. It turned out that she spent her days off visiting her boyfriend in a nearby town and was not happy at the thought of missing three weekends with him.

HOUSE RULES

You should set up house rules as soon as your live-in helper arrives; some may in fact already be part of her contract, but go over them again.

Telephone. Many families had horror stories about the long distance bills their live-in helpers had rung up. Others mentioned that they found it impossible to check in during the day because the helper was constantly on the phone. On the other hand, the helpers mentioned how isolated they felt at home all day with a child. For them, the phone was an important means of keeping in touch with the world.

Our impression is that to restrict a live-in helper's use of the telephone too severely is bad for her morale. But you do have an obligation both to yourself and her to work out the financial and logistical arrangements ahead of time. One mother we talked to felt strongly that a live-in helper should have her own telephone and line. That way, she has access to a phone during both working and nonworking hours without inconveniencing the family.

If you don't want to go to the expense of putting in a new phone line, you will probably want to put some restrictions into practice. Most live-in helpers we interviewed were not allowed to receive any phone calls (except for emergencies, of course) after 10 P.M. They were asked to limit on-duty phone calls to ten minutes. Policies on long distance varied; some families paid part or all of the bill, others paid none. We recommend a long distance allowance, particularly if your helper is from out of town. Once she's past the limit, however, she must pay for her own calls.

Visitors. You should decide how you feel about your live-in helper's friends visiting her during the day, or about other helpers bringing their children over to your house. This can be good for both the helpers and the children, giving adults and kids a break from one another while the children remain supervised and happily occupied. On the other hand, you may be concerned about people you may not have met visiting in your house. One obvious solution is to arrange to meet the people she wants to invite, and to go with her once to the homes she wants to visit. An informal network of mother's helpers and children can be a blessing to all concerned, as long as you are comfortable with how your children are spending their time and how your home is being used.

In any case, your live-in helper will undoubtedly want to develop a network of friends with whom she can socialize in the evening. You may want to limit the number of guests she may have at one time and/or the number of evenings she may have guests in. Some families set a curfew for work nights or a time at which any guest she may have in your home must leave. Others allow the use of her own judgment as long as she is alert and ready for work the next morning. If arrivals and departures are likely to disturb the rest of the family, a curfew is probably wise. In practice, most live-in helpers prefer to do their socializing out of the home.

Boyfriends can present a special problem both logistically and emotionally. You may not feel comfortable having your live-in helper entertain a man in her room, particularly if you have children at an "impressionable" age. And while a nanny in love is probably a happy nanny, the situation will deteriorate rapidly if she and her beau begin having problems in their relationship. Such emotional upheaval will affect your relationship to her and hers with the child. She may turn to you for advice, and you'll have to decide how comfortable you are in the role of confidante.

Use of the car. Using the car is an important aspect of socializing in many areas, so decide ahead of time whether or not you plan to give your live-in helper "off-duty" use of your car. If you decide to restrict that use, keep in mind the extent to which you may be cutting off her social life. One live-in helper recalled a family that lived in a sprawling southern California neighborhood. "They thought they were being generous by giving me most week nights off—but what could I do with the time? Without a car, all I could do was sit in my room, watch television, or talk on the phone." Even if your area has public transportation, forcing your live-in helper to be dependent upon it may not be wise. Suburban buses and trains may not run where she wants to go and may not be that safe late at night. You do not want your helper to feel like a prisoner in your house.

If you do allow her the car for personal use, make some arrangements with her regarding insurance. Some families ask that their live-in helper be responsible for the deductible should she be found at fault in an accident that occurred on personal time. (See Chapter Seven for more on auto insurance.)

CONFERENCES

Every family we spoke to stressed the need for regular times when problems could be discussed and information shared between parents and their live-in helpers. Both welcomed the chance to talk about the child. Either side may have complaints, suggestions, or questions that need to be discussed; so having a regular time to talk means that minor problems can get worked out before they're so big there's no avoiding an explosion. It also means that your talks are less likely to be gripe sessions and more likely to be productive. In most families these "conferences" arise naturally and frequently from the simple inquiry, "Tell me what you did today."

SCHEDULING

Even with a detailed contract, there is a temptation with live-in help to assume that because they are in your house twenty-four hours a day, they're also constantly on call. Live-in helpers and mothers both stressed the importance of making plans well in advance and of being flexible and courteous about last minute changes. You and your live-in helper should decide how many nights she is to be on call for baby-sitting and how far in advance she must be notified as to which nights those will be.

Live-in helpers also mentioned that it is important for parents to call if there are going to be any changes in their daily schedules that will affect their child. "It used to drive me crazy," said one nanny. "I'd make plans to take Jill to the zoo and get her all excited, and then her mother would show up at the last minute and want to take her shopping." Another mother used to "surprise" her au pair by coming home for lunch, and she expected the child to join her even if she'd just been put down for a nap. A little common sense and courtesy will allay most of these problems.

THE EMOTIONAL LIFE
OF YOUR HOUSEHOLD

So far we've talked about the logistical nuts and bolts of having live-in help, but there are some subtle emotional issues that come into play as well. Probably the most important of these is also the simplest, and that is your attitude toward the person you've hired.

If you are overridden with guilt about hiring someone to do your housework and care for your child, you are likely to be unclear about your expectations—and almost certain to be resentful afterward. On the other hand, if you are overly demanding, critical, or unwilling to allow your live-in helper any independent judgment, you are likely to have a frustrated and resentful employee on your hands—and in your house.

"They treated me like the maid" is the line we heard over and over again from unhappy live-in helpers. If this is your attitude toward your live-in help, you are destined for failure. Families who had developed the best relationships with their helpers didn't take the position that they were doing them a favor by letting them live and work "in such a nice house."

Parents and live-in helpers constantly stressed the need for mutual respect and trust. Remember that your children will be extremely sensitive to your attitudes. You can't expect your child to have respect and affection for her nanny, if she doesn't sense that same feeling coming from you. Mary, who was working in Chicago, told us a story that made this point very clearly. It seems that Mary's "child" had a playmate, Louise, who liked to sing. When Mary told Louise that her own nanny had a pretty voice and could perhaps teach her some songs, the little girl replied as disdainfully as only a three-year-old can, "Oh, I'd *never* sing for *Ellen!*" Louise's response didn't really surprise Mary, since Ellen had been complaining for weeks that Louise's parents "treated her like dirt."

The younger your live-in helper the more important it will be to make her feel like part of the family. The happiest young helpers we interviewed (and consequently the happiest parents) were those who felt included in the emotional life of the family. If you want a cooler, more distant relationship with your live-in helper, hire a professional or at least an older woman with more experience.

JEALOUSY

One mother put it bluntly: "I was just plain jealous. It was hard enough for me to leave Diane and go back to work. I couldn't stand to see her so happy with someone else."

Happily, this attitude is unusual. Most mothers, though they reported slight pangs of jealousy, were happy that their children loved and were loved by the helper. "Since I can't be there," said one mother, "I feel better knowing there is someone else there who adores my child." And although they acknowledged some fears of being displaced, all agreed that in fact this had not happened. Their children knew perfectly well who the real parents were, and as one mother put it, "Emily went through a stage where only Nessa could put her to bed, but a month later only Mom would do."

Some live-in helpers we interviewed were indeed fired because they had become too involved with the child. Generally speaking, however, this was the fault of the parent. One helper told us that she had seen many mothers who were uncomfortable with the infant, letting the mother's helper do almost everything for the child at that age. Then, as the child reached an age with which the mother felt more comfortable, the mother tried to establish a relationship. "It's always hard," the woman told us, "and I think it's hard on the baby too." Another nanny had worked for a professional couple who generally left before the child was up and arrived home after she had been put to bed. After six months, she was fired because the child had become too attached to her. "What did they expect?" she asked us. "They were never there."

Mothers and live-in helpers suggested that parents keep some important part of child care for themselves both to avoid jealousy and to lay the foundation for a later relationship. Some parents make a point of calling home at a regular time each day. Others set aside a special time before supper or before bedtime for the child to talk about her day. Another mother had no special routine but said that her children knew how to reach her at work and often called "just to talk." The best situations we encountered were those in which both the live-in helper and the parents spoke highly of each other's involvement with the child.

GIVING YOUR LIVE-IN HELPER
AUTHORITY

Though you will certainly give her guidance, your live-in helper will need to feel free to work out her own relationship with your child. One problem that helpers mentioned frequently was their sense that their authority with the child was being undercut. One astute mother understood this: "You cannot give her responsibility and then take it away whenever it suits you." An au pair who had been instructed not to give any snack after four-thirty in the afternoon was faced several times a month with the specter of the "magnanimous mommy" who swooped in at a quarter to six with a "special treat."

Likewise, if your child rushes to you with a story about what Nanny wouldn't let him do, remind the child that Nanny is in charge when you are not home. Then discuss the matter privately with her. She will appreciate your respect, and the child will learn that the two of you can't be played off against each other.

In this regard it's also important that parents present a united front. We talked to more than one live-in helper who had left her family because of conflicts between the husband and wife. If the parents are having problems, the live-in helper is not going to solve them and it is totally unfair to put her in the middle.

LONELINESS AND HOMESICKNESS

As you might expect, this is a particularly difficult issue with "imported" live-in helpers. We did talk to some parents who didn't feel it was their problem—"She took the job, she knew what she was getting into." But if she's unhappy, she's going to leave, so it *is* your problem. You have a responsibility to help her feel at home in her new community.

The simplest solution is one we've already mentioned: that is, introduce her to other mother's helpers in your neighborhood. There are, moreover, other ways to meet people. Many families encourage their helpers to take courses at nearby community colleges and adult education centers. If your helper is interested in sports, find out about adult leagues, or perhaps there's a nearby health club. The point is that you should help her investigate and pursue her outside interests. Some families pick up the bills for these activities, a nice gesture but not a universal one by any means.

Several agencies that placed out-of-state live-in helpers had an additional recommendation. They suggested arranging an "enforced savings" plan with your helper, withholding anywhere from twenty to forty dollars from her salary for the first ten weeks of employment. The money is placed in an interest-bearing account, and it's returned to her at the end of her year. If she leaves early (without good reason), she forfeits the money. Should you decide to implement such a plan, make sure your live-in helper understands and agrees to it; it should be part of your contract.

WHEN THINGS AREN'T WORKING OUT

Time and good communication solves many problems. It may take your helper longer to catch on to your routines than you had expected; she may need more guidance than you'd hoped; she may be a little homesick; you may feel the loss of privacy more than you had anticipated. If you and she basically like one another, however, it is worth giving yourselves a few months to work things out.

We did talk to some mothers, unfortunately, who knew within the first couple of weeks—in some cases, the first few days—that there was "no way." Their live-in helpers were "lazy," "impatient with their children," "terribly moody," "achingly homesick and weepy," "rigid," "so sloppy they were picking up after them," and so on. All of these mothers reported that they let things go on too long before firing the helper. Their advice: "Cut your losses, don't subject your family to two months of misery when your stomach is gnawing after two weeks."

There are, however, those problems that sneak up quietly. We talked to families who began to suspect drug or alcohol abuse or even stealing. This was particularly difficult for those parents who genuinely liked their helper. Many wanted to help, some going so far as to attend Ala-non meetings or drug abuse counseling. But these parents found that their involvement was too draining and that ultimately their first responsibility was to their child. "As much as I wanted to, I just didn't feel I could trust her anymore," said one mother. Clearly when that basic trust erodes, the situation is untenable and the live-in helper must go.

We did not talk to or hear of any families who had had a problem with child abuse of any kind, but its consequences can be so devastating that the possibility must be mentioned.

If you suspect that any kind of child abuse or neglect is taking place, encourage your child to talk to you. Create as many opportunities as possible to observe the live-in helper with your child. Drop by your home unexpectedly, or arrange for a friend or neighbor to do so. Listen to any complaints your child may have, no matter how vague, and take note of any fears that he or she may have of being left with or touched by the helper. If your suspicions are aroused to such a degree that you feel you cannot trust her—again, let her go.

WHEN YOUR LIVE-IN HELPER LEAVES

If the experience with your live-in helper has been unpleasant, your child will probably be just as glad as you to see her go. But he or she will probably share your trepidations as well about hiring a new live-in helper, so you will have to prepare your child carefully for this.

It will be more difficult for the child if the relationship with the helper has been a satisfying and happy one. Many parents reported that their children blamed themselves for the disappearance of a familiar and beloved figure. Some mothers found that their children became angry and disruptive, others became withdrawn and refused to respond to the next au pair for a time.

Child guidance counselors offer the same advice in this situation as they do for coping with other losses in a child's life. If you can talk the situation out with your child and help him or her express feelings and concerns, the child will have an easier time. You should explain that he or she is not responsible for the helper's leaving and that she still cares about him or her. You might want to hire other sitters for an afternoon even while the helper is still there; that way your child will have a chance to see that other adults can care for him or her as well. If possible, arrange for a gradual transition. Perhaps your live-in helper can come back for visits, or for an occasional evening of babysitting. If your live-in helper is returning to her hometown, a few long-distance phone calls may be in order. Some parents encouraged their children to write to their nanny, but they stressed the importance of first making certain the nanny would be willing to write back.

A number of departing live-in helpers became very involved in the search for their replacement. "My family is so wonderful, I wanted to be sure they got somebody really good," said one girl who was leaving to get married. Others echoed that response, with many adding that it was extremely difficult for them to leave their "second family" even if it was for such attractive reasons as college or marriage.

Clearly the relationship between a live-in helper and her family can be extremely satisfying and rewarding and its impact can last far longer than the time they actually live together. One former live-in helper still attends birthday celebrations for her "kids" and remarked wistfully, "The oldest is talking about college now; I can't be that old."

Seven

Your Financial and Legal Responsibilities

Chances are, in hiring a full-time mother's helper or nanny, you'll be an employer for the first time. If that's the case, you'll no doubt be asking yourself dozens of questions about the financial and legal obligations you're about to incur. How do I determine her wages? Should I charge for room and board? Is it advisable to pay my care giver off the books? What taxes will I have to pay? What benefits should I offer?

Many parents—even those who negotiate office contracts with ease—find ironing out similar agreements with their live-in helper time-consuming, embarrassing, or even trifling. But don't allow yourself to fall into that trap. A clear financial arrangement made at the outset, establishing the time commitment, specifications of wages, precise responsibilities of both parties, and benefits you'll provide will pave the way for a smooth relationship.

This chapter will equip you with all financial and legal information that you'll need to know, so that you and your prospective live-in helper can negotiate an equitable salary arrangement with a minimum of hidden upsets later on.

EVERYTHING YOU WANTED TO KNOW ABOUT WAGES

The Fair Labor Standards Act of 1982 is quite specific. "Casual" baby-sitters do not baby-sit as a vocation, they work intermittently, and their work for all their employers does not come to more than twenty hours a week. You are not required to pay a "casual" baby-sitter the minimum wage.

Any care giver whose work exceeds twenty hours a week for one or more employers is considered full-time and by law must be paid the minimum wage.

Though live-in care givers are subject to the minimum wage act, they are not covered under the Fair Labor Standards Act with provisions for overtime. It is generally agreed that it is difficult to determine how many hours they work since their workplace is also temporarily their home. Any reasonable agreement between the two parties is usually acceptable, but you should put the agreement in writing. The National Committee on Household Employment (NCHE) has developed a code of standards governing overtime for child care workers. The NCHE recommends time and a half for the live-in helper engaged in employment over forty-four hours per week and the same for the live-out care giver employed for more than forty hours per week.

Some states go further than the Fair Labor Standards Act in their stipulations on overtime requirements for live-in child care. The Industrial Welfare Commission of California's labor department does require overtime wages for live-in employees. California's wage board limits the hours of live-in workers to nine hours a day and five days a week; hours worked beyond this must be paid at time and a half.

We talked to many parents who were unclear as to "how much credit" they could take for providing room and board. The government does allow a reasonable deduction from your helper's wages for this, but it is not as much as you might think. An official we talked to at the Federal Department of Labor told us that the calculations on the value of the room and board must be the value to the employer, not to the employee. In other words, you can't say, "Well, if she had to go out and rent a room and buy her own food it would cost her at least two hundred and fifty dollars a month." Instead, you have to calculate the appropriate share of the cost to you. Your accountant may have other suggestions as to how to do this, but some families figure the value of the live-in helper's room as a percentage of the total square footage of their house. Whatever method you use, explain to your prospective live-in helper how you came up with your figures. Do not under any circumstances try to get out of paying a salary by giving an inflated value to room and board.

Once again, the California commission provides guidelines for the amount of credit for meals and lodging that can be used as an offset against the employer's minimum wage obligations. For a room occupied alone, they allow a $16 credit against wages per week, and for a shared room, a $13 offset against weekly wages is permitted. The commission's allowance for meals is $5.05 per day—$1.20 for breakfast, $1.65 for lunch, and $2.20 for dinner. It is required that the lodging be available for full-time occupancy, meaning that it must be available to the child care person seven days of the week. This stipulation has been made to ward off abuse of employers who would erode the minimum wage by providing lodging for five days and require that the helper provide her own lodging for her days off. Deductions for meals and lodgings are not permissible without a voluntary written agreement between the live-in employee and her employer.

In practice, pay rates for live-in child care workers fall into three general levels. The following are rough guidelines that you should find helpful in determining how much your nanny or mother's helper should be paid.

A beginner may be someone new in the country with little or no English and no paid child care experience, or she may be a high school graduate or college-age girl on her first job. The pay rate for these mother's helpers or au pairs is between $75 and $150 per week.

At the intermediate level, the person may have two to five years' experience but be only moderately fluent in English, or another may have some paid child care experience and total English fluency. Standard pay for those at the intermediate level is from $150 to $200.

Any child care worker with over five years' paid experience or any person who has completed specialized training, such as having attended a nanny school, is categorized as a professional. The pay rate for a professional nanny ranges from $200 to $300 or more per week.

Take into account your budget and your needs, and then consider the factors that determine your live-in helper's weekly pay scale. Assess the previous experience of the person you plan to hire and her competence for each task. Is she English-speaking? Can she and will she do the tasks that you need done? Which extra duties will you require in addition to child care? How many children will be under her care? Are they in school for part of the day? Does she drive? Does she have her own car?

Rates for live-in child care also vary depending on geographical area. Make inquiries of your friends and neighbors as to the going rate where you live. The director of the Rent-A-Mom Agency in Denver opened our eyes to how much wages for live-in helpers vary from state to state. His agency caters to middle-income families and has branches in Portland, Syracuse, and Anchorage and he places untrained live-in helpers. In Syracuse his helpers earn $400 a month, in Denver and Portland $550 to $600, and in Anchorage his untrained helpers command a whopping $800 to $1,000 monthly.

Your arrangements for overtime payments should be clarified beforehand. Those mothers we interviewed who employed young women as live-in helpers generally followed similar policies regarding overtime. The salaried work week included five full days plus two or three evenings of baby-sitting. For anything beyond two or three evenings, the woman was ordinarily paid standard baby-sitting rates.

Don't forget to specify the method of payment. More than one employer has been caught in the sticky wicket of presenting a check to a household employee who was expecting cash. Also make clear how often you intend to pay your helper. The usual pay period is once a week; should you decide to pay monthly, remember that a month has 4.3 weeks.

States may differ in their guidelines concerning days off for your live-in helper, so be aware of your own state's regulations in these matters. Everyone we interviewed gave their helpers two twenty-four-hour days off per week. Some employers gave days off back to back, while others split them up. Certain states do require the days off to be consecutive, and some employment agencies stipulate the same. Generally it is more considerate to give a block of time.

There seems to be some personal latitude with the number of sick days, paid holidays, and vacation time that are considered acceptable. We found the number of sick days given varied from four to six per year. The majority of people interviewed provided one week of paid vacation (apart from the family) after the first year of employment and two weeks after two or more years, and it was universally agreed upon that vacation days be clarified well in advance. For example, you should decide if your helper's vacation time should coincide with your own.

Provide six to eight paid holidays per year and make the dates specific. Don't be unexpectedly left in the lurch New Year's Eve, or find out that you have an unhappy conscript for Thanksgiving.

ON THE BOOKS OR OFF?

To some people, under-the-table cash payments are a great temptation when faced with the extra costs and forms required by the government. But not only are off-the-book payments illegal, they probably won't save you that much money in the long run. What's more, there may be hidden bombshells in paying a live-in care giver unreported cash, as is illustrated by a sad story related to us by a mother from Memphis.

The woman hired a mother's helper on a trial basis for a week. During this time the girl invited her boyfriend over to tour the house during a dinner party, spent one full afternoon napping, and showed the children how to roll a joint. The unhappy mother fired the girl, assuming that she had seen the worst and the last of it. But her indignant former employee sued for severance pay and minimum wage violation. It became a nightmare of entanglements with the labor board. As the Memphis woman calculated it, considering the time the girl had actually worked, she had been paid handsomely—well above the minimum wage—but they had had no written agreements.

Even if your employee begs to be paid off the books, when culpability is assessed, it is your responsibility to follow the guidelines for minimum wages and taxes. To the government, "But she wanted to be paid off the books" just isn't a valid argument.

Even if you avoid the short-term legal ramifications, you may find yourself in hot water long after your children are grown, when your live-in sitter of yesteryear applies for Social Security and the IRS unearths no records. Back taxes, interest, and penalties, which are nearly 50 percent, for a bygone live-in helper can be an unpleasant drain when the kids are in college. There is no statute of limitations on Social Security taxes you've failed to pay. Twenty years later, when your by-then senior citizen helper lists you as a former employer, the government will require the taxes, plus heavy fines.

There are also practical and ethical reasons for paying your child care worker on the books. Not providing these basic benefits may turn out to be penny wise and pound foolish. You run the risk of a higher turnover and lower job satisfaction, as well as your own possible guilt over your role as exploitative employer.

We can't emphasize enough that you should respect your child care worker for her vocation. This is, after all, her living, and it is your responsibility to treat your employee fairly.

As a practical matter, most employers of illegal aliens do not report their employee's earnings. Even if a live-in helper's status is legalized in the future, she cannot collect Social Security for the work performed when she worked illegally. If you hire a legal alien as a helper, her status is the same as that of a U.S. citizen, and you are required to pay her Social Security, whether or not she wants you to.

If you hire your helper through an agency, off-the-book payments are generally out of the question.

A THUMBNAIL SKETCH OF TAXES YOU'LL HAVE TO PAY

First, the good news. You can get a tax credit for child care if you and your spouse are employed or looking for employment and you pay someone for the care of children under fifteen.

To determine whether or not you are eligible for a tax credit on child care expenses, go over these rules:

- Both you and your spouse must be gainfully employed or looking for work.
- Your dependents must be children under fifteen.
- You must be paying at least half the cost of maintaining your household.
- You must keep records of all your expenses related to child care and of all wages paid.
- You must make the necessary payroll deductions and pay the unemployment taxes.
- Your child care employee must furnish you with a Social Security account number.
- You must record wages paid to your child care person for duties other than direct dependent care, such as cooking, cleaning, or driving.

Payments for child care are determined by a sliding scale. The top credit for child care is currently $720 for one child and $1,140 for two or more. A number of factors determine the actual amount of your credit—your income, the amount of your child care expenses, and the number of your qualifying children. For the complete rules and changes in the child care tax credit allowances, consult Federal Income Tax Form 2441.

The good news of a child care credit will offset the

disconcerting news that the taxes you can expect to pay for your live-in helper will add a thousand dollars or more to your total child care tab.

To expedite matters and lessen your burden at tax time, be sure to keep good records. Apply to the Internal Revenue Service for a Federal Employer Identification Number (EIN). At the same time, request the Employer's Tax Guide, which you will find packed with helpful information for the first-time employer. To make state-related deductions, you'll also need to apply for a State Employer Identification Number.

In some states you are required to give your child care person a copy of the deductions you take out of each paycheck. In your local stationery store you can purchase a book of blank records called "Statement of Earnings," which will help you keep accurate records. The time you spend in tax matters related to your child care expenses will be considerably shortened if you have a clear understanding of which taxes you must pay, the filing deadlines, and the forms you'll need.

Plan to contend with four types of taxes: Social Security (FICA), Withholding Tax, Unemployment Insurance, and Workers' Compensation.

IRS Form 942, Employer's Quarterly Tax Return for Household Employees, will take care of your Social Security and Withholding Tax obligations. At the point you pay your care giver more than fifty dollars in a quarter, those wages are subject to Social Security tax. Technically, both parties—you and your live-in helper—pay a share of that tax. In 1986 the FICA tax rate was 7.15 percent for each party—a total of 14.30 percent. Some employers we spoke to paid the entire amount themselves; this can be a negotiating point. To derive the amount of the tax, multiply 7.15 percent by your helper's weekly salary, then multiply that resulting number by fifty-two weeks, and you'll arrive at the figure you owe for FICA taxes for one year's full-time work. If you are also paying your helper's share of the Social Security taxes, be sure to double the entire amount of the figure you've come up with. Tax rates may change from year to year, so make sure you obtain the proper schedules.

On the same 942 form, you report any income that is withheld. The law does not require the employer to withhold any income, but if both of you agree that income taxes are to be withheld, the employee should fill out a W-4 form to claim the withholding allowances. From your state tax office, obtain a copy of Publication 15, Circular E for the table of taxes you are to withhold. And remember you must also pay state and local withholding taxes.

Your first tax-related deadline of the year is January 28. By that date you must furnish your employee with Copy B of a W-2 form, on which you've listed the wages paid to her and the FICA and income taxes you have withheld for the previous year. She will need this for her own tax return. Copy A of that form, along with a W-3 form (Transmittal of Income and Tax Statements), must be filed with the government by February 28.

Your federal unemployment (FUTA) insurance liabilities require Form 940. If your full-time employee received a thousand or more dollars in salary for any quarter of the preceding or current year, you must pay federal jobless insurance. The amount varies according to where you live, but for most states the rate is 0.8 percent of the first seven thousand dollars of wages.

State jobless taxes are a separate issue, and again the rates and the base upon which taxes are paid vary considerably from state to state. The amount you pay into the state unemployment funds, however, can often be claimed as a credit against your federal jobless tax. We suggest that you contact the unemployment compensation division of your state labor department for more specific information. Generally, though, you can estimate that federal and state taxes will add about three to four hundred dollars to your child care bill.

For your obligations concerning Workers' Compensation and Disability, place a call to your insurance agent or the state office that runs the compensation program. There is no general rule of thumb. The laws governing compensation and disability insurance are different in almost every state, and in some states your live-in helper may be exempt. In other states, such as New York, the employer is required to carry a policy for both Workers' Compensation and Disability for any household worker who is employed forty or more hours per week. In Connecticut, Workers' Compensation coverage is required for your care giver who works more than twenty-six hours weekly, but no Disability insurance whatsoever is required. New Jersey is different still. There, regardless of the hours an employee works, her employer is obliged to provide Workers' Compensation coverage.

An official in the claims department at Traveler's Insurance gave us some background on Workers' Compensation insurance. Under Workers' Compensation, if an employee is injured on the job, she is automatically covered for those injuries; there is no need to prove liability or negligence. In this sense Workers' Compensation is the original no-fault insurance plan. On the contrary, under your Homeowner's Policy (or tenant's policy, if you are an apartment dweller) the injured party would have to sue you and prove negligence in order to collect damages. This is an important distinction to make, especially if you are paying an employee off the books.

Let's take an example. Say you live in a state that requires Workers' Compensation, but because you are paying "off the books," you do not purchase it. Your live-in helper is subsequently injured in your home and sues you for damages. You call your insurance agent, thinking that your homeowner's policy will cover the claim. Think again. Insurance companies have investigators, and if they are the least bit suspicious that the injured party was not a visitor, but an employee, they will investigate—your neighbors, your children's teachers, and so forth. So ask yourself, would you want a neighbor to perjure himself on your behalf? If the investigator discovers that the claim is being made by an *employee* in a state that requires Workers' Compensation, the company will not honor the claim. You will be personally liable. If your state doesn't require Workers' Compensation, your insurance company won't concern itself with the legality of your live-in helper's status and will determine the validity of payment like any other claim.

We were surprised to learn that illegal aliens are subject to the same Workers' Compensation laws as is anyone else. Employers are obligated to make contributions for them, even if the employers are not paying any other taxes. Actually, every insurance representative we spoke to suggested the purchase of Workers' Compensation even if it's not required. As one broker put it, "It's cheap, and it totally removes the possibility of personal liability."

As you can see, different state regulations run the gamut in requirements, or lack of them, regarding Compensation. To make matters even more confusing, there are several different methods of obtaining Workers' Compensation Insurance. In some states you must pay into a state fund, while in others you may be able to add a special rider to your homeowner's policy. We can't emphasize enough the need for inquiring into what your own state mandates, and then discussing it with your insurance agent.

Organization is the key to dealing efficiently with the extra complexities of child care taxes. If you compile all the forms that you will need for the year, are aware of the deadlines for filing the returns, and calculate an added lump for your child care related taxes, you'll find that the emotional burden and the time spent will be only a small part of your yearly tax bite.

MEDICAL INSURANCE

We were amazed by how many families avoid the issue of health insurance for their live-in helpers. Many skirt this issue by saying they will personally cover any potential medical bills. This is particularly dangerous; your helper's bout with a burst appendix could put you at the door of the poorhouse. In the process of your negotiations, you and your live-in helper can probably work out some arrangement. Perhaps the two of you could share part of the cost for her Blue Cross/Blue Shield. If you hire her through an agency or school, some kind of health benefits will probably be required.

Though it's not entirely aboveboard, if you have a small business or a business at home, you might get away with paying your live-in helper's wages through the business and putting her on that medical plan. It's a good idea to be prepared to show that she does some work for the business, whether it be maintenance or clerical work. With a home office, her cleaning tasks would constitute business employment.

Before you take on the added expense of medical insurance, be sure to ask your helper if she's covered under a family policy—some policies cover offspring up until the age of twenty-five. With her permission, you may want to write to her parents for that information and perhaps offer to make some sort of contributions for them to extend their coverage to include her.

There is some chance that a foreign worker may be covered by a national health policy, but she is probably better off getting a health policy from a U.S. carrier. In New York State, for example, anyone—a citizen or noncitizen—can get a Blue Cross/Blue Shield policy so long as that person has a local address. Most of the mothers we spoke with did not provide more than the basic medical coverage for their live-in helpers. It is neither customary nor expected for you to pay for your helper's dental insurance or to provide eyeglasses.

AUTOMOBILE INSURANCE

Automobile insurance is another matter of concern. Though you should check with your agent about the particulars of your policy, acquiring this coverage probably won't require any extra payments. Standard automobile insurance policies cover your car, no matter who is driving, as long as that person is driving it with your permission.

If you are allowing your live-in helper to have personal use of your car, you may want to make special arrangements covering that situation. Some helpers we talked to had agreed to pay the deductible should they be found at fault in an accident that occurred "off duty." Though this was not a common arrangement, it is worth considering.

BONUSES AND RAISES

You can fashion your policy on bonuses in much the same way you design your own tipping practices. The general range of bonuses given during the holiday season depends on your finances and the extent of your appreciation. Customs also vary from community to community. Take a poll of your friends with live-in helpers. Our guess is that you'll find the bonuses vary from one day's to one week's wages.

Most employment agencies suggest a salary review after six months, and many mothers agree. Raises range from 5 to 10 percent and are considered a good investment. It's vital to remember that as your live-in child care worker's experience increases, so does her earning power. If you plan to be together for more than a year, raise an inexperienced mother's helper or au pair every six months for recognition of that experience. In a short time you'll find that her practical experience will have made an ingenue mother's helper into an experienced professional nanny.

DRAWING UP A CONTRACT

As we've tried to impress, a contract can relieve a lot of the emotional difficulties of hiring someone to work in your home, freeing both sides from guilt, defensiveness, or resentment. A good contract will make both you and your live-in helper aware of each one's rights and responsibilities toward each other. It should detail everything that can reasonably be specified; other areas of concern that can't be spelled out in writing can at least be discussed verbally.

The contract should include most, if not all, of the following types of information:

- The date.
- The full name of your employee.
- Her Social Security number.
- Your full name.
- Your address.
- The names of your children.
- The length of her commitment.
- Her basic hours.
- Her base salary.
- Any overtime provisions.
- Her days off.
- All vacation, sick days, holidays.
- The method and frequency of payment.

- Provisions for taxes, Workers' Compensation, Disability, and Unemployment Insurance.
- Medical insurance and other benefits.
- Your salary review policy.
- Her specific household duties, other than child care, and the number of times per week they are to be done.

You would be wise to make your "household rules" a part of your contract (for more information on these, see Chapter Six):

- Use of car/auto insurance.
- Living conditions.
- Curfews.
- Telephone policy.
- Guest policy.
- Provisions for return travel payment or reimbursement.
- Reasons for termination of employment.

The format of the contract is unimportant; it might be a list or a letter—formal or informal—whatever you and she are most comfortable with. Just make certain that both of you sign the agreement and that each of you keeps a copy. This document, and the respect that it implies, is the key to establishing and maintaining a good relationship.

Appendix and Forms

INFORMATION AND REFERRAL SERVICES

CALIFORNIA CHILD CARE RESOURCE AND REFERRAL NETWORK, 809 Lincoln Way, San Francisco CA 94122, (415) 661-1714. This organization publishes a *national* information and referral directory which you can obtain by sending twenty dollars to the above address. It was updated in the fall of 1986.

COMMUNITY HEALTH SERVICES OF MID-MICHIGAN, 4248 Beecher Road, Apartment B, Flint, MI 48504, Carol Hunt, (313) 762-2088. This is a *national* service.

CHILD CARE INFORMATION SERVICE (CCIS), National Association for the Education of Young Children, 1834 Connecticut Avenue N.W., Washington, D.C. 20009-5786, (202) 232-8777, (800) 424-2460. This organization can provide you with a personalized search for information, but it asks that, before you contact them, you:

- Narrow your question or topic so that it is very specific.
- Identify your purpose for requesting the information.
- Phrase your question to give their computer as many clues as possible to the types of answers you want.
- Include your name, address, and telephone number.

CORPORATE CHILD CARE ORGANIZATIONS

The following organizations work with companies to provide on-site and off-site child care.

CORPORATE CHILD CARE CONSULTANTS, LTD., Suite 500, 741 Piedmont Avenue N.E., Atlanta, GA 30308, (404) 892-0689

KINDER-CARE LEARNING CENTERS, INC., P.O. Box 2151, 2400 President's Drive, Montgomery, AL 36197, (205) 277-5090

WORK/FAMILY DIRECTIONS, 200 The Riverway, Boston, MA 02215, (617) 734-0001

NANNY SCHOOLS

Those schools marked with an (*) are full members of the American Council of Nanny Schools; those marked with a (+) are provisional members.

Arizona

DEVELOPMENT CENTER FOR NANNIES, Kathy Parker, 500 E. Thomas, Phoenix, AZ 85012, (602) 279-3067

California

*AMERICAN NANNY PLAN, INC., Beverly Benjamin, Ph.D., P.O. Box 790, Claremont, CA 91711, (714) 624-7711

AMERICAN SCHOOL OF MOTHERCRAFT NURSING, INC., Mildred Senensieb, M.A., Dean, Suite 204, 19562 Ventura Boulevard, Tarzana, CA 91356, (818) 343-4001

*CALIFORNIA NANNY COLLEGE, Carolyn R. Curtis, Suite 129, 2740 Fulton Avenue, Sacramento, CA 95821, (916) 484-0163

THE GOVERNESS AGENCY/GOVERNESS TRAINING CEN-

TER, Celia Lee Vanoni, #405, 465 Cass Street, San Diego, CA 92109, (619) 270-8311

*CHILD CARE SPECIALISTS CENTER, INC., Sandra Lewis, 9533 Brighton Way, Beverly Hills, CA 90210, (213) 274-2653

THE NANNY INSTITUTE, INC., Jeanne Holst, Director, 6242 Plymouth, San Jose, CA 95129, (408) 257-0304

Colorado

NATIONAL ACADEMY OF NANNIES, INC. (NANI), Terri Eurich, Director, Suite 302, 3665 Cherry Creek Drive North, Denver, CO 80209, (303) 333-6264

Georgia

THE ORIGINAL NANNIES UNLIMITED, Janis Doty, 2300 Peachford Road, Atlanta, GA 30338, (404) 451-0936

Illinois

NANNY U., Pat Kovar, Linda Polk, 2253 Giddings, Chicago, IL 60625, (312) 334-2269

Iowa

CHILD CARE SERVICES, Pat Otis, Supervisor, Kirkwood Community College, P.O. Box 2069, 6301 Kirkwood Boulevard S.W., Cedar Rapids, IA 52406, (319) 398-5411

Kentucky

MIDWAY COLLEGE, Kay Emerson-Roy, Early Childhood Center, Midway, KY 40347, (606) 846-4421

Massachusetts

+NEW ENGLAND SCHOOL FOR NANNIES, Karen Hamlin, 41 Baymore Drive, East Longmeadow, MA 01028, (413) 525-1861

Michigan

*DELTA COLLEGE, Joy Shelton, University Center, MI 48710, (517) 686-9417

Minnesota

*NANNY CHILD CARING PLAN, INC., Jacqueline Richardson, Ph.D., Business and Technology Center, 511 Eleventh Avenue South, Minneapolis, MN 55415, (617) 375-0435

New Jersey

*SHEFFIELD SCHOOL, Ellyn Sheffield, Box 98, Route 518, Hopewell, NJ 08525, (609) 737-8211

Ohio

*NORTH AMERICAN NANNIES, INC., Judith Bunge, Ph.D., 61 Jefferson Avenue, Columbus, OH 43215, (614) 228-6264

*ENGLISH NANNIES SCHOOL, INC., Sheilagh Roth, University Circle, 11206 Euclid Avenue, Cleveland, OH 44106, (216) 231-1515

+NANNIES OF CLEVELAND, INC., Monica Bassett, R.N., 15707 Detroit Avenue, Lakewood, OH 44107, (216) 521-4650

+CHILD CARE PROFESSIONALS INC., Mount St. Joseph College, 5701 Delhi Road, Cincinnati, OH 45051, (513) 561-4810

Oregon

NANNY ACADEMY NORTHWEST, Ann Swindle-Schneider, 5188 S.W. Baird, Portland, OR 97219, (503) 244-0470

*NORTHWEST NANNIES INSTITUTE/NNI PLACEMENT AGENCY, Carolyn Kavanaugh, 2100 N.E. Broadway, Portland, OR 97232, (503) 284-1240

Pennsylvania

+COMMUNITY COLLEGE OF ALLEGHENY COUNTY, Center North, 1130 Perry Highway, Pittsburgh, PA 15237, (412) 366-7000

Texas

TEXAS ACADEMY OF NANNIES, Cheryl Johnson Lee, Director, P.O. Box 1058, Missouri City, TX 77489, (713) 696-8210

*CAPE CENTER, INC., Judith Schneider, Ph.D., Madeline Ehlert, M.Ed., Suite 216, 5924 Royal Lane, Dallas, TX 75230, (214) 692-0263

Washington

*CERTIFIED NANNY PROGRAM, Gloria Myre, M.S.W., Seattle Central Community College, 1701 Broadway, Seattle, WA 98122, (206) 587-6900

EMPLOYMENT AGENCIES

Agencies marked with an (*) are from a list provided by, but not endorsed by, the American Council of Nanny Schools. Agencies marked with a (+) were recommended to us by parents and/or were particularly helpful to us.

Alaska

+RENT-A-MOM, #1222 3605 Arctic Boulevard, Anchorage, AL 99503

California

+WESTON'S DOMESTIC EMPLOYMENT AGENCY, Suite #18, 8230 Beverly Boulevard, Los Angeles, CA 90048, (213) 274-9228

+ANDERSON-LEWIS AGENCY, Helaine Esterson, M.S.W.,

9533 Brighton Way, Beverly Hills, CA 90210, (213) 274-2653

*PROPER NANNIES, LTD., Christine Kerr, 24926 Arnold Drive, Sonoma, CA 95476, (707) 996-5529, (national placement)

Colorado

+RENT-A-MOM, Suite 208, 11000 East Yale, Denver, CO 80014, (303) 671-7011

+STARKEY & ASSOCIATES, INC., Household Professionals, Mary L. Starkey, Suite 307, 222 Milwaukee Street, Denver, CO 80206, (303) 394-4904, (national placement)

Connecticut

*+HELPING HANDS, INC., Sharlene Martin, 33 Whipple Road, Wilton, CT 06897, (203) 834-1742

*+OVERSEAS CUSTOM-MAID AGENCY, Alan Wildstein, 300 Bedford Street, Stamford, CT 06901, (203) 324-9575, (national service)

*HELP!, Doris Elliott, President, 15 Bridge Road, Weston, CT 06883, (203) 226-3456, (203) 226-4200

THE NANNY CONNECTION, Robin Sweet, 21 Livingston Street, New Haven, CT 06511, (203) 787-0611

Georgia

+VERSATILE CARE, Julia Manner, Suite A, 6649 Peachtree Industrial Boulevard, Norcross, GA 30092, (404) 446-7175

*ABC ATLANTA BEST CARE, Beverly Knapton, 3154 Shallow Ford Road, Atlanta, GA 30341, (404) 452-7669, (404) 451-2884

Illinois

*NANNY U., INC., Pat Kovar/Rachel Lee, 2253 Giddings, Chicago, IL 60625, (312) 334-2269

Iowa

EXTRA HANDS, Linda Duran, P.O. Box 631, Marion, IA 52302, (319) 377-5634, (national placement)

Massachusetts

+GALLAGHER AND LABRECQUE AGENCY, Wellesley Square, 568 Washington Street, Wellesley, MA 02181, (617) 235-1552

*CHILD-CARE PLACEMENT SERVICE, INC., Allene Fisch, 149 Buckminster Road, Brookline, MA 02146, (617) 566-6294

+*NEW ENGLAND NANNIES, INC., Karen Hamlin, 41 Baymore Drive, East Longmeadow, MA 01028, (413) 525-1861, (national placement)

*THE CHILD CARE CONNECTION, Donna Coulombe/Michelle Cummings, 27 Wareland Road, Wellesley Hills, MA 02181, (617) 237-7330, (Boston, Washington, D.C., New York placements)

*NANNY SERVICE, Judy Lee Shapiro, 33 Kinnicutt Road, Worcester, MA 01602, (617) 755-9284

*PROFESSIONAL NANNY, INC., Anne Merchant, Executive Director, 354 Washington Street, Wellesley, MA 02181, (617) 237-0211

*AMERICAN NANNY SERVICE, Sherron Carson, 21 Vicksburg Circle, Holden, MA 01520, (617) 757-6151

*ONE ON ONE, INC., Rex Moon, President, 10 Berkley Lane, Andover, MA 01810, (617) 794-2035

Michigan

*GROSSE POINTE EMPLOYMENT, Dolores Andreini, Manager, 18514 Mack Avenue, Grosse Pointe Farms, MI 48236, (313) 885-4576

*+NANNY PROGRAM, Joy Shelton/Vickie Von Steenhouse/Diane Knott, Delta College, University Center, MI 48710, (517) 686-9543

Minnesota

+NANNIES UNLIMITED, INC., Shirley Stuart, 1014 Medical Arts Building, Duluth, MN 55802, (218) 722-1520, (national placement)

New Jersey

*APPLE PIE, Mary Clurman, 67 Upper Mountain Avenue, Montclair, NJ 07042, (201) 746-7813

New York

+AUSTIN EMPLOYMENT AGENCY, 71-09 Austin Street, Forest Hills, NY 11375-4720, (718) 268-2700

+FINNISH EMPLOYMENT AGENCY, Virginia Muhlberg, 206 East 85th Street, New York, NY 10028, (212) 288-6562

+FOX AGENCY, Rita Kirschner, Room 1109, 30 East 60th Street, New York, NY 10022, (212) 753-2686

+PAVILLION AGENCY, Glenn Scott, 15 East 40th Street, New York, NY 10017, (212) 889-6609

*CUSTOM CHILDCARE SERVICES, Lynne Schwartz, Ed.D., 30 West Nyack Village Square, West Nyack, NY 10994, (914) 638-2085

North Carolina

*WAKE UP FOR CHILDREN, Lynne W. Myers, Executive Director, Suite 208, 103 Enterprise Street, Raleigh, NC 27607, (919) 821-0482

Ohio

*APPLE OF YOUR EYE, Christine Fairfield, 7713 Cooper Road, Cincinnati, OH 45242, (513) 793-4880

*CHILD CARE PROFESSIONALS, INC., 6576 Madeira Hills, Cincinnati, OH 45243, (513) 561-4810

Oregon

+RENT-A-MOM, #282, 5331 Southwest MacAdam, Portland, OR 97201, (503) 222-5779

Pennsylvania

*MARGIE SOCKEL, 135 Rebecca Drive, Pittsburgh, PA 15237

Texas

*MOMS, INC., Billie Smith, Suite 215, 2901 Wilcrest, Houston, TX 77042, (713) 975-1105, (national placement)
*NANNIES AND SUCH, INC., Pat Simpkins, 3306 Ivy Falls Drive, Houston, TX 77068, (713) 440-3711, (national placement)

Utah

+NANNIES PLACEMENT SERVICES, 1200 Beneficial Life Tower, 36 South State Street, Salt Lake City, UT 84111, (801) 538-2121, (801) 538-2122, (national placement)
+NANNIES PLACEMENT SERVICES, Box 711-B, Route 2, Heber City, UT 84032, (801) 654-2133, (national placement)

Washington

+RENT-A-MOM, 4526 11th Avenue N.E., Seattle, WA 98105, (206) 547-4080
THERESA SNOW EMPLOYMENT SERVICES INC., Suite 212, Plaza Center Building, 10900 N.E. 8th, Bellevue, WA 98004, (206) 455-1100

BRITISH NANNY SCHOOLS

CHILTERN NURSERY TRAINING COLLEGE, 16 Peppard Road, Caversham, Reading, Berks RG4 8JZ, England

NORLAND NURSERY TRAINING COLLEGE, Denford Park, Hungerford, Berks RG17 0PQ, England

THE PRINCESS CHRISTIAN COLLEGE, 26 Wilbraham Road, Fallowfield, Manchester M14 6JX, England

For more information write

THE NATIONAL NURSERY EXAMINATION BOARD, Argyle House, 29-31 Euston Road, London NW1 2SD, England

THE SCOTTISH NURSERY NURSES' EXAMINATION BOARD, 38 Queen Street, Glasgow G1 3DY, Scotland

British Agencies Placing Nannies and Au Pairs

ALBERMARLE NANNIES, 138 New Bond Street, London W1 Y 9FB, England

BELGRAVIA BUREAU, 35 Brompton Road, Knightsbridge, London SW3 1PW, England

OCCASIONAL AND PERMANENT PLACEMENT AGENCY, 15 Beauchamp Place, Knightsbridge, London SW3 1NQ, England

U.S. GOVERNMENT APPROVED AU PAIR PROGRAMS

AUPAIR*HOMESTAY USA, Mary Brady, Director, Suite 1100, 1522 K Street N.W., Washington, D.C. 20005, (202) 371-9410

AU PAIR IN AMERICA, U.S. Headquarters, American Institute for Foreign Study Scholarship Foundation, Lauren Kratovil, Director, 100 Greenwich Avenue, Greenwich, CT 06830, (203) 869-9090, Telex: 5101009715 AIFS INBOUND

EUROPEAN HEADQUARTERS, J. Robert Atkinson, Director, 37 Queens Gate, London SW7 5HR, England, 01-581-2733, Telex: 25357

IMMIGRATION AND LABOR CERTIFICATION INFORMATION

IMMIGRATION AND NATURALIZATION SERVICE (INS), 425 I Street N.W., Washington, D.C. 20536, (202) 633-2000 (main switchboard), (202) 633-2648 (public information office)

Regional Labor Certification Offices

I. *Boston*
   Connecticut
   Maine
   New Hampshire
   Rhode Island
   Vermont
   J. F. Kennedy Building, Boston, MA 02203, (617) 223-7328

II. *New York*
   New Jersey
   New York
   Puerto Rico
   Virgin Islands
   Room 3701, 1515 Broadway, New York, NY 10036, (212) 944-3214

III. *Philadelphia*
   Delaware
   Maryland
   Pennsylvania
   Virginia
   Washington, D.C.
   West Virginia
   P.O. Box 8796, Room 13300, 3535 Market Street, Philadelphia, PA 19101, (215) 596-6363

IV. *Atlanta*
Alabama
Florida
Georgia
Kentucky
Mississippi
North Carolina
South Carolina
Tennessee
Room 405, 1371 Peachtree Street N.E., Atlanta, GA 30367, (404) 347-3938

V. *Chicago*
Illinois
Indiana
Michigan
Minnesota
Ohio
Wisconsin
Room 634, 230 South Dearborn Street, Chicago, IL 60604, (312) 353-1549

VI. *Dallas*
Arkansas
Louisiana
New Mexico
Oklahoma
Texas
Room 317, Federal Building, 525 Griffin Street, Dallas, TX 75202, (214) 767-4975

VII. *Kansas City*
Iowa
Kansas
Missouri
Nebraska

Room 700, 911 Walnut Street, Kansas City, MS 64106, (816) 374-6411

VIII. *Denver*
Colorado
Montana
North Dakota
South Dakota
Utah
Wyoming
Room 1676, 1961 Stout Street, Denver, CO 80294, (303) 844-4143

IX. *San Francisco*
Arizona
California
Guam
Hawaii
Nevada
Room 9108, 450 Golden Gate Avenue, San Francisco, CA 94102, (415) 556-5624

X. *Seattle*
Alaska
Idaho
Oregon
Washington
Room 1136, Federal Office Building, 909 First Avenue, Seattle, WA 98174, (206) 442-5297

NEWSPAPERS RECOMMENDED FOR CLASSIFIED ADVERTISING

MILWAUKEE *Journal,* Box 661, Milwaukee, WI 53201, (414) 224-2000
MINNEAPOLIS *Star & Tribune,* 425 Portland Avenue, Minneapolis, MN 55488, (612) 372-4141

PORTLAND *Press Herald,* 390 Congress Street, Portland, ME 04104, (207) 775-5811

GRAND FORKS *Herald,* 114-120 North Fourth Street, Grand Forks, ND 58201, (701) 775-4211

The Deseret News, P.O. Box 45838, Salt Lake City, UT 84145, (801) 237-2775

THE SALT LAKE *Tribune,* P.O. Box 45838, Salt Lake City, UT 84145, (801) 237-2775

The Irish Echo, 309 Fifth Avenue, New York, NY 10016, (212) 686-1266

The International Herald Tribune, 850 Third Avenue, New York, NY 10022, (212) 752-3890

Application for Employer Identification Number

Form SS-4
(Rev. November 1985)
Department of the Treasury
Internal Revenue Service

Application for Employer Identification Number

(For use by employers and others. Please read
the separate instructions before completing this form.)

For Paperwork Reduction Act Notice, see separate instructions.

OMB No 1545-0003
Expires 8-31-88

1 Name (True name See instructions)

2 Social security no., if sole proprietor

3 Ending month of accounting year

4 Trade name of business if different from item 1

5 General partner's name, if partnership, principal officer's name, if corporation, or grantor's name, if trust

6 Address of principal place of business (Number and street)

7 Mailing address, if different

8 City, state, and ZIP code

9 City, state, and ZIP code

10 Type of organization
☐ Governmental
☐ Individual ☐ Trust
☐ Nonprofit organization
☐ Partnership
☐ Corporation
☐ Plan administrator
☐ Other (specify)

11 County of principal business location

12 Reason for applying
☐ Started new business
☐ Purchased going business
☐ Other (specify)

13 Acquisition or starting date (Mo., day, year) See instructions

14 Nature of principal activity (See instructions)

15 First date wages or annuities were paid or will be paid (Mo., day, year).

16 Peak number of employees expected in the next 12 months (If none, enter "0") ▶
☐ Nonagricultural
☐ Agricultural
☐ Household

17 Does the applicant operate more than one place of business?
☐ Yes ☐ No

18 Most of the products or services are sold to whom?
☐ Business establishments (wholesale)
☐ General public (retail)
☐ Other (specify)
☐ N/A

19 If nature of business is manufacturing, state principal product and raw material used.

20 Has the applicant ever applied for an identification number for this or any other business?
☐ Yes ☐ No
If "Yes," enter name and trade name. Also enter approx date, city, and state where the application was filed and previous number if known ▶

Under penalties of perjury, I declare that I have examined this application, and to the best of my knowledge and belief it is true, correct, and complete

Signature and Title ▶

Date ▶

Telephone number (include area code)

Please leave blank ▶ | Geo. | Ind | Class | Size | Reas. for appl.

Part I

Employer's Quarterly Tax Return for Household Employees

Form 942
(Rev. January 1986)
Department of the Treasury
Internal Revenue Service

Employer's Quarterly Tax Return for Household Employees
(For Social Security and Withheld Income Taxes)

OMB No. 1545-0034
Expires 9-30-88

Your name, address, employer identification number, and calendar quarter of return. (If not correct, please change.)

Name

Address and ZIP code

Date quarter ended

Employer identification number

If address is different from prior return, check here ☐

FOR IRS USE ONLY

1 1 1 1 1 1 1 1 1 2 2 2 2 2 2 2 2 2 3 3 3 3 3

4 4 5 6 7 7 7 7 7 8 8 8 9 1 0 0 0 0 0 0 0 0 0 0

Social security taxes are due for each household employee to whom you paid cash wages of $50 or more in the calendar quarter covered by this return. For income tax withholding, see page 2.

		Dollars	Cents
1	Total cash wages		
2	Social security taxes (multiply line 1 by 14.3% (.143))		
3	Federal income tax withheld (if requested by your employee)		
4	Total taxes (add lines 2 and 3)		
5	Advance earned income credit (EIC) payments, if any (see Notes below)		
6	Total taxes due (subtract line 5 from line 4) Pay to the Internal Revenue Service		

If you will **NOT** need to file Form 942 in the future, check here ☐   If no tax is due, write **NONE** on line 6.

Important: Form W-2 must be given to each employee and filed with the Social Security Administration—see page 4.

Under the penalties of perjury, I declare that I have examined this return, and to the best of my knowledge and belief it is true, correct, and complete.

Signature of employer ▲

Date ▲

Employee's Withholding Allowance Certificate

Form **W-4**
(Rev. January 1986)

Department of the Treasury—Internal Revenue Service

Employee's Withholding Allowance Certificate

OMB No. 1545-0010
Expires 11-30-87

1 Type or print your full name

2 Your social security number

Home address (number and street or rural route)

3 Marital Status

☐ Single ☐ Married

☐ Married, but withhold at higher Single rate

Note: If married, but legally separated, or spouse is a nonresident alien, check the Single box.

City or town, state, and ZIP code

4 Total number of allowances you are claiming (from line F of the worksheet on page 2)

5 Additional amount, if any, you want deducted from each pay · · · · · · $

6 I claim exemption from withholding because (see instructions and check boxes below that apply):

a ☐ Last year I did not owe any Federal income tax and had a right to a full refund of ALL income tax withheld, AND

b ☐ This year I do not expect to owe any Federal income tax and expect to have a right to a full refund of ALL income tax withheld. If both a and b apply, enter the year effective and "EXEMPT" here ▶ 19 ___ Year

c If you entered "EXEMPT" on line 6b, are you a full-time student? · · · · · · ☐ Yes ☐ No

Under penalties of perjury, I certify that I am entitled to the number of withholding allowances claimed on this certificate, or if claiming exemption from withholding, that I am entitled to claim the exempt status.

Employee's signature ▶ Date ▶ ___, 19 ___

7 Employer's name and address (Employer: Complete 7, 8, and 9 only if sending to IRS)

8 Office code

9 Employer identification number

Wage and Tax Statement

1 Control number		OMB No. 1545-0008		
2 Employer's name, address, and ZIP code			3 Employer's identification number	4 Employer's State number
			5 Statutory employee ☐ Deceased ☐ Legal rep ☐ 942 emp ☐ Subtotal ☐ Void ☐	
			6 Allocated tips	7 Advance EIC payment
8 Employee's social security number	9 Federal income tax withheld		10 Wages, tips, other compensation	11 Social security tax withheld
12 Employee's name, address, and ZIP code			13 Social security wages	14 Social security tips
			16	
			17 State income tax	18 State wages, tips, etc	19 Name of State
			20 Local income tax	21 Local wages, tips, etc	22 Name of locality

form **W-2 Wage and Tax Statement** 1985   Copy 1 For State, City, or Local Tax Department ☐
Employee's and employer's copy compared

Transmittal of Income and Tax Statements

OMB No. 1545-0008

1 Control number				
Kind of Payer and Tax Statements Transmitted	2 941/941E ☐ CT-1 ☐ Military ☐ 942 ☐ 943 ☐ Medicare Fed emp ☐		3 W-2 ☐ W-2P ☐	4	5 Number of statements attached
6 Allocated tips	7 Advance EIC payments		8		
9 Federal income tax withheld	10 Wages, tips, and other compensation		11 Social security tax withheld		
12 Employer's State number	13 Social security wages		14 Social security tips		
15 Employer's identification number ———			16 Establishment number		
17 Employer's name			18 Gross annuity, pension, etc. (Form W-2P)		
YOUR COPY			20 Taxable amount (Form W-2P)		
19 Employer's address and ZIP code			21 Income tax withheld by third-party payer		

Form **W-3** Transmittal of Income and Tax Statements **1985**

Department of the Treasury
Internal Revenue Service

Employer's Annual Federal Unemployment Tax Return

Form **940**	**Employer's Annual Federal Unemployment (FUTA) Tax Return**	OMB No 1545 0028
Department of the Treasury Internal Revenue Service	▶ For Paperwork Reduction Act Notice, see page 2.	**1985**

	Name (as distinguished from trade name)	Calendar Year		T
If incorrect, make any necessary change. ▶		1985		FF
	Trade name if any	Employer identification number		FD FP
	Address and ZIP code			I T

A Did you pay all required contributions to your state unemployment fund by the due date of Form 940? (If none required check No) ☐ Yes ☐ No

If you checked the Yes box, enter amount of contributions paid to your state unemployment fund ▶ $

B Are you required to pay contributions to only one state? ☐ Yes ☐ No

If you checked the Yes box (1) Enter the name of the state where you are required to pay contributions ▶

(2) Enter your state reporting number(s) as shown on state unemployment tax return ▶

Part I Computation of Taxable Wages and Credit Reduction (To Be Completed by All Taxpayers)

1 Total payments (including exempt payments) during the calendar year for services of employees | 1

2 Exempt payments (Explain each exemption shown, attaching additional sheets if necessary) ▶ .... Amount paid

3 Payments for services of more than $7,000. Enter only the excess over the first $7,000 paid to individual employees not including exempt amounts shown on line 2. Do not use the state wage limitation | 2

4 Total exempt payments (add lines 2 and 3) | 4

5 Total taxable wages (subtract line 4 from line 1) (If any part is exempt from state contributions, see instructions) ▶ | 5

6 Credit reduction for unpaid advances to the states listed (by 2 letter Postal Service abbreviations). Enter the wages included on line 5 above for each state and multiply by the rate shown (See the instructions)

							Outside the United States
(a) CT	x 007	(e) OH	x 008				
(b) IL	x 009	(f) PA	x 009	(i) PR	x 006		
(c) LA	x 006	(g) VT	x 006	(j) VI	x 0.2		
(d) MN	x 011	(h) WV	x 008				

7 Total credit reduction (add lines 6(a) through 6(j) and enter in Part II, line 2 or Part III, line 4) ▶ | 7

Part II Tax Due or Refund (Complete if You Checked the "Yes" Boxes in Both Questions A and B Above).

1 FUTA tax. Multiply the wages in Part I, line 5, by 008 and enter here | 1

2 Enter amount from Part I, line 7 | 2

3 Total FUTA tax (add lines 1 and 2) | 3

4 Less Total FUTA tax deposited for the year, including any overpayment applied from a prior year (from your records) | 4

5 Balance due (subtract line 4 from line 3—if over $100, see Part IV instructions). Pay to IRS ▶ | 5

6 Overpayment (subtract line 3 from line 4) Check if it is to be Applied to next return, or Refunded ▶ | 6

Part III Tax Due or Refund (Complete if You Checked the "No" Box in Either Question A or B Above. Also complete Part V)

1 Gross FUTA tax. Multiply the wages in Part I, line 5, by 062 | 1

2 Maximum credit. Multiply the wages in Part I, line 5, by 054 | 2

3 Enter the smaller of the amount in Part V, line 11, or Part III, line 2 | 3

4 Enter amount from Part I, line 7 | 4

5 Credit allowable (subtract line 4 from line 3) (If zero or less, enter 0) | 5

6 Total FUTA tax (subtract line 5 from line 1) | 6

7 Less Total FUTA tax deposited for the year, including any overpayment applied from a prior year (from your records) | 7

8 Balance due (subtract line 7 from line 6—if over $100, see Part IV instructions). Pay to IRS ▶ | 8

9 Overpayment (subtract line 6 from line 7) Check if it is to be Applied to next return, or Refunded ▶ | 9

Part IV Record of Quarterly Federal Tax Liability for Unemployment Tax (Do not include state liability)

Quarter	First	Second	Third	Fourth	Total for Year
Liability for quarter					

If you will not have to file returns in the future, write "Final" here (see general instruction "Who Must File") and sign the return ▶

Under penalties of perjury, I declare that I have examined this return, including accompanying schedules and statements, and to the best of my knowledge and belief it is true, correct and complete, and that no part of any payment made to a state unemployment fund claimed as a credit was or is to be deducted from the payments to employees.

Signature ▶   Title (Owner, etc.) ▶   Date ▶

Form **940** (1985)

Credit for Child and Dependent Care Expenses

Form **2441**	**Credit for Child and Dependent Care Expenses**	OMB No 1545-0058
Department of the Treasury Internal Revenue Service (O)	▶ Attach to Form 1040. ▶ See Instructions below.	19**85** 23

Name(s) as shown on Form 1040 — Your social security number

1 Write the number of qualifying persons who were cared for in 1985. (See the instructions below for the definition of qualifying persons.) ▶ **1**

2 If payments listed on line 3 were made to an individual, complete the following.

	Yes	No
a If you paid $50 or more in a calendar quarter to an individual, were the services performed in your home? **2a**		
b If "Yes," have you filed appropriate wage tax returns on wages for services in your home (see the instructions for line 2)? **2b**		

Employer ID number

c If the answer to b is "Yes," write your employer identification number. ▶ **2c**

3 Write the amount of qualified expenses you incurred and actually paid in 1985 for the care of the qualifying person, but do not write more than $2,400 ($4,800 if you paid for the care of two or more qualifying persons). **3**

4 You must write your earned income on line 4c. See the instructions for line 4 for the definition of earned income.

• If you were unmarried at the end of 1985, write your earned income on line 4c, OR

• If you are married, filing a joint return for 1985, you must complete lines 4a and 4b.

a Write your earned income **4a**

b Write your spouse's earned income **4b**

c Compare amounts on lines 4a and 4b, and write the smaller of the two amounts on line 4c. **4c**

5 Compare amounts on lines 3 and 4c, and write the smaller of the two amounts on line 5 **5**

6 Write the percentage from the table below that applies to the adjusted gross income on Form 1040, line 33. **6**

If line 33 is:		Percentage is:	If line 33 is:		Percentage is:
Over—	But not over—		Over—	But not over—	
$0–10,000		30% (.30)	$20,000–22,000		24% (.24)
10,000–12,000		29% (.29)	22,000–24,000		23% (.23)
12,000–14,000		28% (.28)	24,000–26,000		22% (.22)
14,000–16,000		27% (.27)	26,000–28,000		21% (.21)
16,000–18,000		26% (.26)	28,000		20% (.20)
18,000–20,000		25% (.25)			

7 Multiply the amount on line 5 by the percentage shown on line 6, and write the result. **7**

8 Multiply any child and dependent care expenses for 1984 that you paid in 1985 by the percentage that applies to the adjusted gross income on Form 1040, line 33, for 1984. Write the result. (See line 8 instructions for the required statement.) **8**

9 Add amounts on lines 7 and 8. Write the total here and on Form 1040, line 41. This is the maximum amount of your credit for child and dependent care expenses **9**

Application for a Social Security Number Card

FORM SS-5 – APPLICATION FOR A SOCIAL SECURITY NUMBER CARD (Original, Replacement or Correction)

Unless the requested information is provided, we may not be able to issue a Social Security Number (20 CFR 422-103(b))

INSTRUCTIONS TO APPLICANT ▶	Before completing this form, please read the instructions on the opposite page. Type or print, using pen with dark blue or black ink. Do not use pencil. **SEE PAGE 1 FOR REQUIRED EVIDENCE.**

1

NAA	NAME TO BE SHOWN ON CARD	First		Middle		Last
NAB	FULL NAME AT BIRTH (IF OTHER THAN ABOVE)	First		Middle		Last
ONA	OTHER NAME(S) USED					

2

| STT | MAILING ADDRESS | (Street/Apt No P O Box, Rural Route No) |
| CTY | CITY (Do not abbreviate) | STE | STATE | ZIP | ZIP CODE |

3 CSP CITIZENSHIP (Check one only)

- a U S citizen
- b Legal alien allowed to work
- c Legal alien not allowed to work
- d Other (See instructions on Page 2)

4 SEX SEX
- ☐ MALE
- ☐ FEMALE

5 ETB RACE/ETHNIC DESCRIPTION (Check one only) (Voluntary)

- a Asian, Asian-American or Pacific Islander (includes persons of Chinese, Filipino, Japanese, Korean, Samoan etc. ancestry or descent)
- b Hispanic (includes persons of Chicano, Cuban, Mexican or Mexican-American, Puerto Rican, South or Central American or other Spanish ancestry or descent)
- c Negro or Black (not Hispanic)
- d Northern American Indian or Alaskan Native
- e White (not Hispanic)

| DOB DATE OF BIRTH ▶ MONTH DAY YEAR | **7** AGE PRESENT AGE | **8** PLB PLACE OF BIRTH | CITY (Do not abbreviate) | STATE OR FOREIGN COUNTRY (Do not abbreviate) | FCI ☐ |

9

| MNA | MOTHERS NAME AT HER BIRTH | First | | Middle | | Last (Her maiden name) |
| FNA | FATHERS NAME | First | | Middle | | Last |

10

PNO a Has a Social Security number card ever been requested for the person listed in item 1? ☐ YES(2) ☐ NO(1) ☐ Don't know(1)   b Was a card received for the person listed in item 1? ☐ YES(3) ☐ NO(1) ☐ Don't know(1)

▶ IF YOU CHECKED YES TO A OR B, COMPLETE ITEMS C THROUGH E; OTHERWISE GO TO ITEM 11.

SSN c Enter the Social Security number assigned to the person listed in item 1

NLC d Enter the name shown on the most recent Social Security card issued for the person listed in item 1

e Date of Birth correction (See instruction 10 on page 2) POB MONTH DAY YEAR

11 DON TODAY'S DATE ▶ MONTH DAY YEAR   **12** Telephone number where we can reach you during the day. Please include the area code ▶ HOME OTHER

ASD WARNING: Deliberately furnishing (or causing to be furnished) false information on this application is a crime punishable by fine or imprisonment, or both.

IMPORTANT REMINDER: WE CANNOT PROCESS THIS APPLICATION WITHOUT THE REQUIRED EVIDENCE. SEE PAGE 1.

13 YOUR SIGNATURE

14 YOUR RELATIONSHIP TO PERSON IN ITEM 1 ☐ Self ☐ Other (Specify)

WITNESS (Needed only if signed by mark "X")   WITNESS (Needed only if signed by mark "X")

DO NOT WRITE BELOW THIS LINE (FOR SSA USE ONLY)

DTC (SSA RECEIPT DATE)	NPN	DOC
NTC	CAN	BIC	IDN	ITV ☐ MANDATORY IN PERSON INTERVIEW CONDUCTED
TYPE(S) OF EVIDENCE SUBMITTED				SIGNATURE AND TITLE OF EMPLOYEE(S) REVIEWING EVIDENCE AND/OR CONDUCTING INTERVIEW
				DATE
			DCL	DATE

FORM SS-5 (1-85) 5/84 edition may be used until supply is exhausted   3

Arrival and Departure Record

U.S. Department of Justice
Immigration and Naturalization Service

OMB No. 1115-0077
Expires 10-31-88

Welcome to the United States

177642686 00

I-94 Arrival/Departure Record - Instructions

This form must be completed by all persons except U.S. citizens, returning resident aliens, aliens with immigrant visas, and Canadian Citizens visiting or in transit.

Type or print legibly with pen in ALL CAPITAL LETTERS. Use English. Do not write on the back of this form.

This form is in two parts. Please complete both the Arrival Record (Items 1 through 13) and the Departure Record (Items 14 through 17).

When all items are completed, present this form to the U.S. Immigration and Naturalization Service Inspector.

Item 7 - If you are entering the United States by land, enter LAND in this space. If you are entering the United States by ship, enter SEA in this space.

Form I-94 (10-01-85)N

Admission Number

177642686 00

Immigration and
Naturalization Service

I-94
Arrival Record

1. Family Name
2. First (Given) Name
3. Birth Date (Day, Mo, Yr)
4. Country of Citizenship
5. Sex (Male or Female)
6. Passport Number
7. Airline and Flight Number
8. Country Where You Live
9. City Where You Boarded
10. City Where Visa Was Issued
11. Date Issued (Day, Mo, Yr)
12. Address While in the United States (Number and Street)
13. City and State

Departure Number

177642686 00

Immigration and
Naturalization Service

I-94
Departure Record

14. Family Name
15. First (Given) Name
16. Birth Date (Day, Mo, Yr)
17. Country of Citizenship

See Other Side   STAPLE HERE

Nonimmigrant (Visitor) Visa Application

1. SURNAMES OR FAMILY NAMES (Exactly as in Passport)	**DO NOT WRITE IN THIS SPACE**
	B-1/B-2 MAX B-1 MAX B-2 MAX
2. FIRST NAME AND MIDDLE NAME (Exactly as in Passport)	OTHER _____ MAX Visa Classification
	MULT OR _____ Number Applications
3. OTHER NAMES (Maiden, Religious, Professional, Aliases)	MONTHS _____ Validity
4. DATE OF BIRTH (Day, Month, Year) 7. PASSPORT NUMBER	ISSUED ON _____ BY _____
	REFUSED ON _____ BY _____
5. PLACE OF BIRTH (City, Province, Country) DATE PASSPORT ISSUED	UNDER SEC. _____ INA
6. NATIONALITY DATE PASSPORT EXPIRES	REFUSAL REVIEWED BY _____
	L.O. CHECKED _____
8. HOME ADDRESS (Include apartment no., street, city, province, and postal zone)	
9. NAME AND STREET ADDRESS OF PRESENT EMPLOYER OR SCHOOL (Postal box number unacceptable)	
10. HOME TELEPHONE NO. 11. BUSINESS TELEPHONE NO.	
12. SEX ☐ Female ☐ Male 13. COLOR OF HAIR 14. COLOR OF EYES	
15. COMPLEXION 16. HEIGHT 17. MARITAL STATUS ☐ Married ☐ Single ☐ Widowed ☐ Divorced ☐ Separated	
18. MARKS OF IDENTIFICATION	
19. NAMES AND RELATIONSHIPS OF PERSONS TRAVELING WITH YOU (NOTE A separate application must be made for a visa for each traveler, including children and infants.)	25. PRESENT OCCUPATION (If retired, state past occupation)
20. HAVE YOU EVER APPLIED FOR AN IMMIGRANT OR NONIMMIGRANT U.S. VISA BEFORE? ☐ No ☐ Yes Where? When? ☐ Visa was issued Type of visa? ☐ Visa was refused	26. AT WHAT ADDRESS WILL YOU STAY IN THE U.S.A.?
21. HAS YOUR U.S. VISA EVER BEEN CANCELED? ☐ No ☐ Yes	27. WHAT IS THE PURPOSE OF YOUR TRIP?
22. Bearers of visitors visas may not work or study in the U.S. DO YOU INTEND TO WORK IN THE U.S.? ☐ No ☐ Yes If YES, explain	28. WHEN DO YOU INTEND TO ARRIVE IN THE U.S.A.?
	29. HOW LONG DO YOU PLAN TO STAY IN THE U.S.A.?
23. DO YOU INTEND TO STUDY IN THE U.S.? ☐ No ☐ Yes If YES, write name and address of school as it appears on form I-20.	30. DO YOU PLAN FUTURE TRIPS TO THE U.S.A.? IF SO, WHEN?
24. WHO WILL FURNISH FINANCIAL SUPPORT, INCLUDING TICKETS?	31. HAVE YOU EVER BEEN IN THE U.S.A.? ☐ No ☐ Yes When? For how long?
NONIMMIGRANT VISA APPLICATION	**COMPLETE ALL QUESTIONS ON REVERSE OF FORM**

OPTIONAL FORM 156 (Rev. 6/82) PAGE 1   50156—106   NSN 7540-00-139-0053
Department of State   PREVIOUS EDITION NOT USABLE

Nonimmigrant (Visitor) Visa Application

32. (a) HAS ANYONE EVER FILED AN IMMIGRANT VISA PETITION ON YOUR BEHALF? (b) HAS LABOR CERTIFICATION FOR EMPLOYMENT IN THE U.S. EVER BEEN REQUESTED BY YOU OR ON YOUR BEHALF? (c) HAVE YOU OR ANYONE ACTING FOR YOU EVER INDICATED TO A U.S. CONSULAR OR IMMIGRATION EMPLOYEE A DESIRE TO IMMIGRATE TO THE U.S.?

(a) ☐ No   ☐ Yes   (b) ☐ No   ☐ Yes   (c) ☐ No   ☐ Yes

33. ARE ANY OF THE FOLLOWING IN THE U.S.? (If YES, circle appropriate relationship and indicate what that person is doing in the U.S., i.e., studying, working, etc.)

HUSBAND/WIFE _____ FIANCE/FIANCEE _____ BROTHER/SISTER _____

FATHER/MOTHER _____ SON/DAUGHTER _____

34. PLEASE LIST THE COUNTRIES WHERE YOU HAVE LIVED FOR MORE THAN 6 MONTHS DURING THE PAST 5 YEARS

COUNTRIES	CITIES	APPROXIMATE DATES

35. IMPORTANT: ALL APPLICANTS MUST READ AND ANSWER THE FOLLOWING:

A visa may not be issued to persons who are within specific categories defined by law as inadmissible to the United States (except when a waiver is obtained in advance). Complete information regarding these categories and whether any may be applicable to you can be obtained from this office. Generally, they include persons

- Afflicted with contagious diseases (i.e., tuberculosis) or who have suffered serious mental illness;

- Arrested, convicted for any offense or crime even though subject of a pardon, amnesty, or other such legal action;

- Believed to be narcotic addicts or traffickers;

- Deported from the U.S.A. within the last 5 years;

- Who have sought to obtain a visa by misrepresentation or fraud;

- Who are or have been members of certain organizations including Communist organizations and those affiliated therewith;

- Who ordered, incited, assisted, or otherwise participated in the persecution of any person because of race, religion, national origin, or political opinion under the control, direct or indirect, of the Nazi Government of Germany, or of the government of any area occupied by, or allied with, the Nazi Government of Germany.

DO ANY OF THESE APPEAR TO APPLY TO YOU?   ☐ No   ☐ Yes
If YES, or if you have any question in this regard, personal appearance at this office is recommended. If it is not possible at this time, attach a statement of facts in your case to this application.

36. I certify that I have read and understood all the questions set forth in this application and the answers I have furnished on this form are true and correct to the best of my knowledge and belief. I understand that possession of a visa does not entitle the bearer to enter the United States of America upon arrival at port of entry if he or she is found inadmissible.

DATE OF APPLICATION _____

APPLICANT'S SIGNATURE _____

If this application has been prepared by a travel agency or another person on your behalf, the agent should indicate name and address of agency or person with appropriate signature of individual preparing form.

SIGNATURE OF PERSON PREPARING FORM _____

DO NOT WRITE IN THIS SPACE

37 mm x 37 mm

PHOTO

Glue or staple photo here

Application for Alien Employment Certification

OMB Approval No. 44-R1301

U.S. DEPARTMENT OF LABOR
Employment and Training Administration

APPLICATION
FOR
ALIEN EMPLOYMENT CERTIFICATION

IMPORTANT: READ CAREFULLY BEFORE COMPLETING THIS FORM
PRINT legibly in ink or use a typewriter. If you need more space to answer questions on this form, use a separate sheet. Identify each answer with the number of the corresponding question. SIGN AND DATE each sheet in original signature.

To knowingly furnish any false information in the preparation of this form and any supplement thereto or to aid, abet, or counsel another to do so is a felony punishable by $10,000 fine or 5 years in the penitentiary, or both (18 U.S.C. 1001).

PART A. OFFER OF EMPLOYMENT

1. Name of Alien (Family name in capital letter, First, Middle, Maiden)

2. Present Address of Alien (Number, Street, City and Town, State ZIP Code or Province, Country)

3. Type of Visa (If in U.S.)

The following information is submitted as evidence of an offer of employment.

4. Name of Employer (Full name of organization)

5. Telephone (Area Code and Number)

6. Address (Number, Street, City or Town, Country, State, ZIP Code)

7. Address Where Alien Will Work (if different from item 6)

8. Nature of Employer's Business Activity

9. Name of Job Title

10. Total Hours Per Week
 a. Basic
 b. Overtime

11. Work Schedule (Hourly)
 a.m.
 p.m.

12. Rate of Pay
 a. Basic $ per
 b. Overtime $ per hour

13. Describe Fully the Job to be Performed (Duties)

14. State in detail the MINIMUM education, training, and experience for a worker to perform satisfactorily the job duties described in Item 13 above.

15. Other Special Requirements

EDU-CATION (Enter number of years)	Grade School	High School	College	College Degree Required (specify)
				Major Field of Study

TRAIN-ING	No. Yrs.	No. Mos.	Type of Training

EXPERI-ENCE	Job Offered		Related Occupation	Related Occupation (specify)
	Number			
	Yrs.	Mos.	Yrs.	Mos.

16. Occupational Title of Person Who Will Be Alien's Immediate Supervisor

17. Number of Employees Alien will Supervise

ENDORSEMENTS (Make no entry in section - for government use only)

Date Forms Received	
L.O.	S.O.
R.O.	N.O.
Ind. Code	Occ. Code
Occ. Title	

Replaces MA 7-50A, B and C (Apr. 1970 edition) which is obsolete.

ETA 750 (Oct. 1976)

Application for Alien Employment Certification

18. COMPLETE ITEMS ONLY IF JOB IS TEMPORARY		19. IF JOB IS UNIONIZED (Complete)	
a. No. of Openings To Be Filled By Aliens Under Job Offer	b. Exact Dates You Expect To Employ Alien	a. Number of Local	b. Name of Local
	From To		c. City and State

20. STATEMENT FOR LIVE-AT-WORK JOB OFFERS (Complete for Private Household Job ONLY)					
a. Description of Residence	b. No. Persons Residing at Place of Employment				c. Will free board and private room not shared with anyone be provided? ("X" one)
("X" one) ☐ House ☐ Apartment	Number of Rooms	Adults	Children	Ages	☐ YES ☐ NO
			BOYS		
			GIRLS		

21. DESCRIBE EFFORTS TO RECRUIT U.S. WORKERS AND THE RESULTS. (Specify Sources of Recruitment by Name)

22. Applications require various types of documentation. Please read PART II of the instructions to ensure that appropriate supporting documentation is included with your application.

23. EMPLOYER CERTIFICATION

By virtue of my signature below, I HEREBY CERTIFY the following conditions of employment.

a. I have enough funds available to pay the wage or salary offered the alien.

b. The wage offered equals or exceeds the prevailing wage and I guarantee that, if a labor certification is granted, the wage paid to the alien when the alien begins work will equal or exceed the prevailing wage which is applicable at the time the alien begins work.

c. The wage offered is not based on commissions, bonuses, or other incentives, unless I guarantee a wage paid on a weekly, bi-weekly or monthly basis.

d. I will be able to place the alien on the payroll on or before the date of the alien's proposed entrance into the United States.

e. The job opportunity does not involve unlawful discrimination by race, creed, color, national origin, age, sex, religion, handicap, or citizenship.

f. The job opportunity is not:

(1) Vacant because the former occupant is on strike or is being locked out in the course of a labor dispute involving a work stoppage.

(2) At issue in a labor dispute involving a work stoppage.

g. The job opportunity's terms, conditions and occupational environment are not contrary to Federal, State or local law.

h. The job opportunity has been and is clearly open to any qualified U.S. worker.

24. DECLARATIONS

DECLARATION OF EMPLOYER ▶ Pursuant to 28 U.S.C. 1746, I declare under penalty of perjury the foregoing is true and correct.

SIGNATURE		DATE
NAME (Type or Print)	TITLE	

AUTHORIZATION OF AGENT OF EMPLOYER ▶ I HEREBY DESIGNATE the agent below to represent me for the purpose of labor certification and I TAKE FULL RESPONSIBILITY for accuracy of any representations made by my agent.

SIGNATURE OF EMPLOYER		DATE
NAME OF AGENT (Type or Print)	ADDRESS OF AGENT (Number, Street, City, State, ZIP Code)	

Application for Alien Employment Certification

PART B. STATEMENT OF QUALIFICATIONS OF ALIEN

FOR ADVICE CONCERNING REQUIREMENTS FOR ALIEN EMPLOYMENT CERTIFICATION: If alien is in the U.S., contact nearest office of Immigration and Naturalization Service. If alien is outside U.S., contact nearest U.S. Consulate.

IMPORTANT: READ ATTACHED INSTRUCTIONS BEFORE COMPLETING THIS FORM.

Print legibly in ink or use a typewriter. If you need more space to fully answer any questions on this form, use a separate sheet. Identify each answer with the number of the corresponding question. Sign and date each sheet.

1. Name of Alien (Family name in capital letters)	First name	Middle name	Maiden name

2. Present Address (No., Street, City or Town, State or Province and ZIP Code	Country	3. Type of Visa (If in U.S.)

4. Alien's Birthdate (Month, Day, Year)	5. Birthplace (City or Town, State or Province)	Country	6. Present Nationality or Citizenship (Country)

7. Address in United States Where Alien Will Reside

8. Name and Address of Prospective Employer if Alien has job offer in U.S.	9. Occupation in which Alien is Seeking Work

10. "X" the appropriate box below and furnish the information required for the box marked

a. ☐ Alien will apply for a visa abroad at the American Consulate in ⟶	City in Foreign Country	Foreign Country
b. ☐ Alien is in the United States and will apply for adjustment of status to that of a lawful permanent resident in the office of the Immigration and Naturalization Service at ⟶	City	State

11. Names and Addresses of Schools, Colleges and Universities Attended (Include trade or vocational training facilities)	Field of Study	FROM		TO		Degrees or Certificates Received
		Month	Year	Month	Year	

SPECIAL QUALIFICATIONS AND SKILLS

12. Additional Qualifications and Skills Alien Possesses and Proficiency in the use of Tools, Machines or Equipment Which Would Help Establish if Alien Meets Requirements for Occupation in Item 9.

13. List Licenses (Professional, journeyman, etc.)

14. List Documents Attached Which are Submitted as Evidence that Alien Possesses the Education, Training, Experience, and Abilities Represented

Endorsements	DATE REC. DOL
(Make no entry in this section — FOR Government Agency USE ONLY)	O.T. & C.

(Items continued on next page)

Application for Alien Employment Certification

15. WORK EXPERIENCE. List all jobs held during past three (3) years. Also, list any other jobs related to the occupation for which the alien is seeking certification as indicated in item 9.

a. NAME AND ADDRESS OF EMPLOYER

NAME OF JOB	DATE STARTED Month	Year	DATE LEFT Month	Year	KIND OF BUSINESS

DESCRIBE IN DETAIL THE DUTIES PERFORMED, INCLUDING THE USE OF TOOLS, MACHINES, OR EQUIPMENT	NO. OF HOURS PER WEEK

b. NAME AND ADDRESS OF EMPLOYER

NAME OF JOB	DATE STARTED Month	Year	DATE LEFT Month	Year	KIND OF BUSINESS

DESCRIBE IN DETAIL THE DUTIES PERFORMED, INCLUDING THE USE OF TOOLS, MACHINES, OR EQUIPMENT	NO. OF HOURS PER WEEK

c. NAME AND ADDRESS OF EMPLOYER

NAME OF JOB	DATE STARTED Month	Year	DATE LEFT Month	Year	KIND OF BUSINESS

DESCRIBE IN DETAIL THE DUTIES PERFORMED, INCLUDING THE USE OF TOOLS, MACHINES, OR EQUIPMENT	NO. OF HOURS PER WEEK

16. DECLARATIONS

DECLARATION OF ALIEN ▶ Pursuant to 28 U.S.C. 1746, I declare under penalty of perjury the foregoing is true and correct.

SIGNATURE OF ALIEN	DATE

AUTHORIZATION OF AGENT OF ALIEN ▶ I hereby designate the agent below to represent me for the purpose of labor certification and I take full responsibility for accuracy of any representations made by my agent.

SIGNATURE OF ALIEN	DATE

NAME OF AGENT (Type or print)	ADDRESS OF AGENT (No., Street, City, State, ZIP Code)

Petition for Prospective Immigrant Employee

U.S. Department of Justice
Immigration and Naturalization Service (INS) **Petition for Prospective Immigrant Employee**   OMB # 1115-0061
Expires 4/88

DO NOT WRITE IN THIS BLOCK

Case ID#	Action Stamp	Fee Stamp
A#		
G-28 or Volag#		
Petition was filed on		Petition is approved for status under section
(Priority Date)		☐ 203(a)(3) ☐ 203(a)(6)
		Section 212(a)(14) certification
		☐ Attached ☐ Sched A. Group _____

A. Information about this petition

This petition is being filed for a: ☐ 3rd Preference immigrant   ☐ 6th Preference immigrant   (See instructions for definitions and check one block only)

B. Information about employer

1. Name (Family name in CAPS) (First) (Middle) or (Company Name)

2. Address (Number and Street)

(Town or City)   (State/Country)   (ZIP/Postal Code)

3. Address where employee will work (if different) (Number and Street)

(Town or City)   (State/Country)   (ZIP/Postal Code)

4. Employer is: ☐ an organization   ☐ a permanent resident
(check one) ☐ a U.S. citizen   ☐ a nonimmigrant

5. Social Security Number   or   INS employer ID number

6. Alien Registration Number (if any)

7. Description of Business (Nature, number of employees, gross and net annual income, date established) (if employer is an individual, state occupation and annual income)

8. Have you ever filed a visa petition for an alien employee in this same capacity?
☐ Yes   ☐ No   (If Yes how many?)

9. Are you and the prospective employee related by birth or marriage?
☐ Yes   ☐ No

10. Are separate petitions being filed at this time for other aliens?
☐ Yes   ☐ No   (If Yes list names)

11. Title and salary of position offered

12. Is the position permanent?   ☐ Yes   ☐ No
13. Is the position full-time?   ☐ Yes   ☐ No
14. Is this a newly-created position?   ☐ Yes   ☐ No
(If No, how long has it existed?)

C. Information about prospective employee

1. Name (Family name in CAPS) (First)   (Middle)

2. Address (Number and Street)   (Apartment Number)

(Town or City)   (State/Country)   (ZIP/Postal Code)

3. Place of Birth (Town or City)   (State/Country)

4. Date of Birth (Mo/Day/Yr)   5. Sex   6. Marital Status
☐ Male   ☐ Married   ☐ Single
☐ Female   ☐ Widowed   ☐ Divorced

7. Other names used (including maiden name)

8. Profession or occupation and years held

9. Social Security Number   10. Alien Registration Number (if any)

11. Name and address of present employer (Name)

(Number and Street)

(Town or City)   (State/Country)   (ZIP/Postal Code)

12. Date employee began present employment

13. If employee is currently in the U.S., complete the following: He or she last entered as a (visitor, student, exchange alien, crewman, stowaway, temporary worker without inspection, etc.)

Arrival/Departure Record (I-94) Number   Date entered (Month/Day/Year)

Date authorized stay expired, or will expire as shown on Form I-94 or I-95

14. Has a visa petition ever been filed by or on behalf of this person?
☐ Yes   ☐ No   (If Yes explain)

INITIAL RECEIPT	RESUBMITTED	RELOCATED		COMPLETED		
		Rec'd	Sent	Approved	Denied	Returned

I-140

Form I-140 (08-01-85) N

Petition for Prospective Immigrant Employee

C. (continued) Information about prospective employee

16. List husband/wife and all children of prospective employee

Name	Relationship	Date of Birth	Country of Birth	Present Address

16. Employee's address abroad

	(Number and Street)	(Town or City)	(Province)	(Country)

17. If your employee's native alphabet is other than Roman letters, write his/her name and address abroad in the native alphabet:

(Name)	(Number and Street)	(Town or City)	(Province)	(Country)

18. Check the appropriate box below and give the information required for the box you checked:

☐ The employee will apply for a visa abroad at the American Consulate in _____ (City) _____ (Country)

☐ The employee is in the United States and will apply for adjustment of status to that of a lawful resident in the office of the Immigration and Naturalization Service at _____ (City) _____ (State). If the employee is not eligible for adjustment of status, he or she will apply for a visa abroad at the American Consulate in _____ (City) _____ (Country)

Warning: The INS investigates employment experience. If the INS finds that employment experience is false, the application is denied and the person responsible for providing false information may be criminally prosecuted.

Penalties: You may, by law, be fined up to $10,000, imprisoned up to five years, or both, for knowingly and willfully falsifying or concealing a material fact or using any false document in submitting this petition.

Your Certification

This petition may only be filed by one of the following:

I am ☐ the employer
☐ the prospective employee (only allowed for 3rd preference)
☐ a person filing on behalf of and authorized by the prospective employee (only allowed for 3rd preference)

I certify, under penalty of perjury under the laws of the United States of America, that the foregoing is true and correct. Furthermore, I authorize the release of any information from my records which the Immigration and Naturalization Service needs to determine eligibility for the benefit that I am seeking.

Print Name _____ Title _____

Signature _____ Date _____ Phone Number _____

Signature of Person Preparing Form If Other than Above

I declare that I prepared this document at the request of the person above and that it is based on all information of which I have any knowledge.

(Print Name)	(Address)	(Signature)	(Date)

G-28 ID Number _____

Voting Number _____

I-140

Application to Extend Time of Temporary Stay

UNITED STATES DEPARTMENT OF JUSTICE IMMIGRATION AND NATURALIZATION SERVICE	READ INSTRUCTIONS CAREFULLY FEE WILL NOT BE REFUNDED	OMB No. 1115 – 0083 Expires 1-84

FEE STAMP

APPLICATION TO EXTEND
TIME OF TEMPORARY STAY

**I HEREBY APPLY TO EXTEND MY
TEMPORARY STAY IN THE UNITED STATES**

PRESS FIRMLY – LEGIBLE COPY REQUIRED. PRINT OR TYPE YOUR NAME EXACTLY AS IT APPEARS ON YOUR ARRIVAL – DEPARTURE RECORD FORM I-94. IF YOUR MAILING ADDRESS IN THE U.S. IS WITH SOMEONE WHOSE FAMILY NAME IS DIFFERENT FROM YOURS, INSERT THAT PERSON'S NAME IN THE C/O BLOCK.

6 DATE TO WHICH EXTENSION IS REQUESTED

1 YOUR NAME | FAMILY NAME (CAPITAL LETTERS) | FIRST | MIDDLE

OR CARE OF | C/O

7 REASON FOR REQUESTING EXTENSION

2 MAILING ADDRESS IN U.S | NUMBER AND STREET (APT. NO.) | FILE NUMBER
CITY | STATE | ZIP CODE

3 DATE OF BIRTH (MO /DAY/YR.) | COUNTRY OF BIRTH | COUNTRY OF CITIZENSHIP

4 PRESENT NONIMMIGRANT CLASSIFICATION | DATE ON WHICH AUTHORIZED STAY EXPIRES | TELEPHONE NUMBER

5 DATE AND PORT OF LAST ARRIVAL IN U.S | NAME OF VESSEL, AIRLINE, OR OTHER MEANS OF LAST ARRIVAL IN U.S

8 REASON FOR COMING TO THE U.S

THE ADMISSION NUMBER FROM MY I-94 IS

FOR GOVERNMENT USE ONLY

☐ EXTENSION GRANTED TO (DATE) | DATE OF ACTION

9 HAS AN IMMIGRANT VISA PETITION EVER BEEN FILED IN YOUR BEHALF?
YES ☐ NO ☐ IF "YES" WHERE WAS IT FILED?

☐ EXTENSION DENIED V.D. TO (DATE) | DD OR OIC OR OFFICE

10 HAVE YOU EVER APPLIED FOR AN IMMIGRANT VISA OR PERMANENT RESIDENCE IN THE U.S.? ☐ YES ☐ NO IF "YES" WHERE DID YOU APPLY?

11 I INTEND TO DEPART FROM THE U.S. ON (DATE)
I AM IN POSSESSION OF A TRANSPORTATION TICKET FOR MY DEPARTURE ☐ YES ☐ NO

12 PASSPORT NO. | EXPIRES ON (DATE) | ISSUED BY (COUNTRY) | 13 NUMBER, STREET, CITY, PROVINCE (STATE) AND COUNTRY OF PERMANENT RESIDENCE

14 MY USUAL OCCUPATION IS | 15 SOCIAL SECURITY NO. (IF NONE, STATE "NONE")

16 I ☐ AM ☐ AM NOT MARRIED IF YOU WISH TO APPLY FOR EXTENSION FOR YOUR SPOUSE AND CHILDREN GIVE THE FOLLOWING (SEE INSTRUCTIONS # 1)

NAME OF SPOUSE AND CHILDREN	DATE OF BIRTH	COUNTRY OF BIRTH	PASSPORT ISSUED BY (COUNTRY) AND EXPIRES ON (DATE)

NOTE: IF SPOUSE AND CHILDREN FOR WHOM YOU ARE SEEKING EXTENSION DO NOT RESIDE WITH YOU GIVE THEIR COMPLETE ADDRESS ON A SEPARATE ATTACHMENT TO THIS APPLICATION

17 I (INSERT "HAVE" OR "HAVE NOT") _____ BEEN EMPLOYED OR ENGAGED IN BUSINESS IN THE UNITED STATES IF YOU HAVE BEEN EMPLOYED OR ENGAGED IN BUSINESS IN THE UNITED STATES, COMPLETE THE REST OF THE BLOCK

NAME AND ADDRESS OF EMPLOYER OR BUSINESS	INCOME PER WEEK	DATES EMPLOYMENT OR BUSINESS BEGAN AND ENDED

I certify that the above is true and correct

SIGNATURE OF APPLICANT | DATE

SIGNATURE OF PERSON PREPARING FORM, IF OTHER THAN APPLICANT

I declare that this document was prepared by me at the request of the applicant and is based on all information on which I have any knowledge.

SIGNATURE | ADDRESS | DATE

ATTACH YOUR FORMS I-94 OR I-144 – "DO NOT SEND YOUR PASSPORT

RECEIVED	TRANS. IN	RET'D TRANS OUT	COMPLETED

Form I-539 (Rev. 6-8-83)N